I Am the Child

USING BRAIN GYM®
WITH CHILDREN WHO
HAVE SPECIAL NEEDS

CECILIA K. FREEMAN, M.ED.
WITH GAIL E. DENNISON

Ed   nia

I Am the Child: Using Brain Gym®
With Children Who Have Special Needs
© 1998 by Cecilia K. Freeman with Gail E. Dennison.
All rights reserved.

Illustrations © 1998 by Gail E. Dennison
Printed in the United States of America
Book design by Sara Patton, Maui, Hawaii

ISBN 0-942143-1018

Published by Edu-Kinesthetics, Inc.
P.O. Box 3395
Ventura, CA 93006-3395

Brain Gym® is a registered trademark, used by permission of the Educational Kinesiology Foundation. Vision Gym™, also referred to in the text of this book, is a pending trademark, also used by permission of the Educational Kinesiology Foundation. *I Am the Child: Using Brain Gym® With Children Who Have Special Needs* has been approved for publication by the Trademark Review Department of the Educational Kinesiology Foundation.

Contents

A Message From the Publisher V

Acknowledgments VII

Foreword VIII

Preface IX

I Am the Child XI

Introduction: How I Became a Special-Education Teacher 1

1. Creating a Safe Environment 7

2. An Introduction to My Students, Who Are
    My Teachers 28

3. Child, Parent, Teacher: A Cooperative Learning Model 45

4. Inviting General-Ed Peers 62

5. Ordering Developmental Priorities 86

6. Honoring the Child's Search for Structure 105

7. Establishing Boundaries 116

8. Reaching Beyond the Familiar 128

9. Bringing Out the Child's Gifts 144

10. Working Through My Own Issues in the Classroom ... 160

Some Closing Words 168

Key Brain Gym Movements 170

Additional Edu-K Processes 189

Bibliography 192

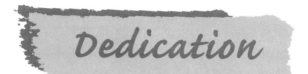

Dedication

*To all my students, who teach me
how to discover my commitment to life
as they give me the opportunity to explore my spirit;
and to all the parents of my students, who learn
to grow with their children's uniqueness.*

A Message From the Publisher

*T*his book has been published by Edu-Kinesthetics, Inc., under the auspices of the Educational Kinesiology Foundation, a nonprofit school in Ventura, California, that offers courses for Brain Gym®, Vision Gym™, and other Educational Kinesiology (Edu-K) processes. The Foundation's President, Paul E. Dennison, Ph.D., is an educator who has over the past twenty-five years introduced an entirely new method of teaching: one that uses body movements to activate whole-brain potential, in the system known as Brain Gym. Gail E. Dennison, creator of the Vision Gym™ course, authors and co-authors courses and manuals with her husband and others.

From beginning to end, this book has been a creative project of love and pride. The parents of the children in Cecilia Freeman's classroom have responded wholeheartedly to the opportunity to share with the world the joy and learning experienced through Brain Gym by these exceptional children. At the parents' request, we have included photos of the children and used their actual names. For reasons of privacy, the names and identifying details of certain other individuals mentioned in the book have been changed.

I Am the Child: Using Brain Gym® With Children Who Have Special Needs tells how a classroom teacher implements, in her own work, the Dennisons' research and professional experience. It is a human-interest story about one teacher's experiences, over a two-year period, in using the Brain Gym movements with her class—one in which the students are profoundly physically, mentally, or emotionally challenged. While this teacher found the movements to be invaluable, the information stated herein is not intended as a prescription. It does, however, raise questions regarding our way of educating children—not just those who have suffered brain damage or physical injury, but children in general. Further information about the use of Brain Gym with children and adults who have special needs can be obtained from the Educational Kinesiology Foundation at the address below.

The Brain Gym method of learning is used in homes, schools, and businesses—for improved performance in academics, sports, and theater arts—in more than thirty countries worldwide. All of the Brain Gym activities referred to are from the book *Brain Gym* by Paul E. Dennison, Ph.D., and Gail E. Dennison, first published in 1986 by Edu-Kinesthetics, Inc.

For more information, for a directory of Brain Gym Instructors in your area, or for a comprehensive description of courses, contact:

The Educational Kinesiology Foundation
Post Office Box 3396
Ventura, CA 93006-3396
Telephone: (800) 356-2109 or (805) 658-7942
Fax: (805) 650-0524
email address: EDUKFD@aol.com
Web site address: www.braingym.com

To order books, please contact:

Edu-Kinesthetics, Inc.
Post Office Box 3395
Ventura, CA 93006-3395
Telephone: (888) 388-9898 or (805) 650-3303
Fax: (805) 650-1689

For descriptions and applications of some of the key Brain Gym and Edu-K activities used in Cecilia Freeman's classroom and referred to throughout this book, see the section entitled "Brain Gym Movements That Enhance Specific Developmental Skills," pages 170 to 191.

Acknowledgments

I offer deep gratitude to Gail Dennison for the hundreds of hours of professional consultation she rendered as I wrote this book. Her skill in providing focus continues to inspire me. The depth, the understanding, and the expansion of the technical information within the body of this work blossomed under Gail's guidance. Her ability to organize the stories and gracefully language the events that occurred has created a loving and coherent presentation of the children in my classroom.

I would also like to acknowledge and thank the following people:

Paul Dennison, who — with his clarity of mind, heartfelt encouragement, and profound understanding of the relationship of movement to learning — continues to believe in my every endeavor of life.

Sonia Nordenson, who provides fine-tuning with her editing and gives me vision to continue to use the Brain Gym work in my classroom.

Marilyn Bouchard Lugaro, who perceived the depth of the work and encouraged me to persevere in the rewriting of challenging sections, offering new perspectives on my format.

Dee Coulter, who offered suggestions for editing and organizing the book.

Wayne Freeman, whose loving support creates a home environment that provides a safe place for me to continue to experience life as an adventure.

All of the colleagues who have offered their support as I pioneer this work with the multiple challenges of the special-needs population.

All of the children and their parents, who continue to touch my life as we share our blessings with one another.

Foreword

I am pleased to recommend this compelling book, *I Am the Child*, by Cecilia Freeman. The book, a collection of personal experiences, is the product of a remarkable teacher who describes how she uses special techniques to help children with special needs. I have personally witnessed the remarkable progress in several of the children described in this book. It is very important to these children to have a teacher with such energy, imagination, and skills. I am glad that she felt it important to put her knowledge into words to share with others.

This book describes a personal journey that is still ongoing. The techniques described are not a quick fix, nor are they appropriate for every child. They are not a cure for brain injury. The book describes a bidirectional teaching technique in which the student and the teacher constantly trade places. Many of the children whose stories are told would not be good candidates for conventional therapies and teaching techniques. In the past, many of them would have been placed in institutions.

The first part of the book focuses on the development of sensitivity and awareness. The author brings this out by quoting a series of "quick writes" from fourth-grade peer tutors. These short notes reflect amazing insight for such young minds. The author expands on this by showing reactions from the mothers of her students. It is rare that a teacher can truly show sensitivity and awareness that can compete with a mother's dedication. Later in the book, the author describes individual students, and even relates how some were able to graduate from her class.

I would consider this work among "the Oliver Sacks school of fascination, observation, and interaction." There is a wonderful feeling of cautious fascination, careful observation, and sensitive interaction throughout the book. Paul and Gail Dennison are remarkable individuals who have many excellent publications that are highly regarded. I welcome this book as an addition to these treasures.

– William D. Goldie, M.D.
Clinical Neurological Services, Camarillo, California

Preface

In my career in education over the past thirty years, I have met, instructed, and supervised hundreds of teachers. I have known loving caregivers, selfless motivators, and inspiring communicators, and I honor all those who give of themselves to nurture the younger generation as it moves through the educational system. Never have I known, however, a teacher with the courage, heart, and creativity of Cecilia Freeman.

Brain Gym has been called another way to say "I love you." With my wife, Gail Dennison, I developed the Brain Gym movements for use with learning-challenged students at my reading centers. Convinced that these children were intelligent, motivated youngsters who simply didn't know how to focus, I found that movement was truly the door to their learning. Working mostly on a one-on-one basis with this population, I discovered specific Brain Gym activities to help with each particular challenge, such as encoding, decoding, comprehension, or organization.

Since then, the Brain Gym system has become internationally known as a way to enhance learning for the average or gifted individual. In educational circles, it has proven to offer revolutionary information. Yet, in private practice, I have had only a few opportunities to work with people who have multiple handicaps, and have never had the responsibility of addressing those challenges in a classroom setting on a continuous basis. In taking Brain Gym to this population, Cecilia Freeman has broken new ground. She has demonstrated the ability to go into a classroom, day after day, and lovingly join with each and every child. Cecilia can get in touch with what each child needs, move with the child, and communicate with the child through love. This is the essence of Brain Gym.

When Cecilia would ask Gail and me, in those first few months of her new teaching assignment, "What should I do with a child who ... ?" we would say, "You need to back up to move forward." We challenged her to adapt our movements to this special-needs population. Cecilia would take on the posture of each particular child for us, acting out patterns of movement so that we could sense the developmental needs. Often we could tell what sensory skill the child was attempting to learn, and would make suggestions for drawing this out.

This was the beginning of Cecilia's exploration. She kept us updated on a weekly basis as she faced new challenges and marked milestones of progress with her kids. It is both validating and encouraging to see how much she has been able to accomplish using Brain Gym for only a few minutes a day with each child. I have met some of these children, and Gail and I know all of their stories. Miracles are indeed made of hard work and determination.

I believe in Cecilia Freeman. I am glad that Gail and I could inspire her in her undertaking. I know that only a teacher with Cecilia's gifts could have done so much with the concepts with which she began.

– Paul E. Dennison, Ph.D.
Co-Founder, the Educational Kinesiology Foundation

I Am the Child

I am the child who cannot talk. You often pity me; I see it in your eyes. You wonder how much I am aware of . . . I see that, as well. I am aware of much: whether you are happy or sad or fearful, patient or impatient, full of love and desire to help me or just doing your duty by me. I marvel at your frustration, knowing mine to be far greater, for I cannot express myself nor my needs as you do. You cannot conceive of my isolation, so complete is it at times. I do not gift you with clever conversation, cute remarks to be laughed over and repeated. I do not give you answers to your everyday questions, responses regarding my well-being, sharing of my needs, or comments about the world around me. I do not give you rewards as defined by the world's standards—great strides in development for which you can credit yourself. I do not give you understanding as you know it.

What I give you instead is so much more valuable . . . I give you opportunities. Opportunities to discover the depth of your character, not mine; the depth of your life, your commitment, your patience, your abilities; the opportunity to explore your spirit more deeply than you imagined possible. I drive you further than you would ever go on your own, working harder, seeking answers to your many questions, creating questions with no answers. I am the child who cannot talk.

I am the child who cannot walk. The world sometimes seems to pass me by. You see the longing in my eyes to get out of this chair, to run and play like other children. There is much that you take for granted. I want the toys on the shelf, I need to go to the bathroom—oh, I've dropped my fork again. I am dependent on you in these ways. My gift to you is to make you aware of your great fortune: your healthy back and legs, your ability to do for yourself. Sometimes people appear not to notice me; I always notice them. I feel not so much envy as desire, desire to stand upright, to put one foot in front of the other, to be independent. I give you awareness. I am the child who cannot walk.

I am the child who is mentally impaired. I don't learn easily, if you judge me by the world's measuring stick. What I do know is infinite joy in the simple things. I am not burdened as you are with the strifes and conflicts of a more complicated life. My gift to you is to grant you the freedom to enjoy things as a child, to teach you how much your arms around me mean, to give you love. I give you the gift of simplicity. I am the child who is mentally impaired.

I am the disabled child. I am your teacher. If you allow me, I will teach you what is really important in life. I will give you and teach you unconditional love. I gift you with my innocent trust, my dependency upon you. I teach you of respect for others and for their uniqueness. I teach you about the sanctity of life. I teach you about how very precious this life is and about not taking things for granted. I teach you about forgetting your own needs and desires and dreams. I teach you giving. Most of all, I teach you hope and faith. I am the disabled child.

Author unknown. Reprinted with the permission of the International Rett Syndrome Association Newsletter, (800) 818-7388.

Introduction

How I Became a Special-Education Teacher

*I*n 1995, I was doing hospice work with the elderly in private homes. One Sunday in August, I picked up the classified section of the newspaper to scan the nursing category for possible clients. Just for fun, and in a spirit of adventure, I turned to the teaching category.

I had previously taught students with special needs, first in Virginia and then in New Hampshire. The learning disorders of these children had been relatively minimal; my students had been labeled as "learning-disabled" and/or "emotionally disturbed." Now here I was, after pursuing other careers for eleven years, pondering the possibility of teaching in California. Reading an advertisement titled "Special Day Class Teacher With Severely Handicapped Students," I said to myself, "Hmmm ... 'special day class' ... what's that? 'severely handicapped' ... what could that mean?"

Images came into my mind of children who were blind, deaf, autistic, in wheelchairs ... physically challenged or emotionally disturbed ...

I thought I'd better stay in the nursing category and continue my hospice work, but after a few minutes I was drawn again to read that ad. Something about the idea of working with such special children touched my very heart and soul. My recent experiences with a body-based learning program known as Brain Gym® and my rediscovery of my own joy in learning had given me a new sense of possibility. By the third time that I went back to the ad, I knew that—even though I had no clear idea what a "special day class" was—I wanted the job.

I updated my resume, established my teaching credentials in California, applied for the job, interviewed for it, and started work two days after the interview.

When I first walked into this Special Day classroom that morning two years ago, it was with a feeling of excitement and enthusiasm—and without a clue as to what my daily life in this room would be like. I thought, "Well, here I am again ... a teacher. Isn't this a funny turn of events? I never thought I'd teach in a classroom again."

In the eleven years since I had left public school teaching, I had operated a massage therapy business, learned to build wooden boats, started my own school to teach "at-risk" young people to build sixteen-foot wooden sailboats, taught yoga classes, worked as a certified nurse's aide, and given home hospice care to the dying. From each experience, I had discovered something more about my own learning process. My most recent work, with the sick, the elderly, and the dying, had brought me to a place of deep faith in the inner rewards of giving my full attention to another person's needs. Now I had come full circle: I was a school teacher, working with children once again.

When I was in the fifth grade, I had a wonderful teacher— Sister Pauline Marie—who influenced me greatly. She was an inspiring woman who always asked her students to find their greatest heart's desire ... to follow their dreams ... to do the necessary work to become a genuine human being, so as to be of service to others. Sister Pauline exemplified her own favorite saying: "Actions speak louder than words."

I grew up in what used to be called a broken home, living with my alcoholic father and seven brothers and sisters.

Although we lived in a middle-class neighborhood, we didn't have much money. Sister Pauline invited me to look beyond the circumstances of my family life, and in responding to her invitation I began a lifelong journey inward.

I questioned everything. I wanted life to be less of a struggle: I wondered how I could change myself to become "like everybody else," and wondered why life felt so hard for me when people all around me seemed to be enjoying it, or at least having an easier time.

At seventeen, in the midst of all these questions and this search for a purpose in life, I took a summer job in a pickle factory. There I met John Mildrew, a kind man who, like Sister Pauline Marie, had great enthusiasm for life. He was a high school physics and calculus teacher who was working a summer factory job. In his conversations with me, Mr. Mildrew offered me the gift of believing in myself. He helped me to see that each day brings a very blessed opportunity; and he helped me to expand my view of the world. So, with John Mildrew's steadfast encouragement, my fifth-grade dream of becoming a teacher resurfaced.

I spent the next two years working as a legal secretary to pay my college expenses. I wanted to bring to fruition the seed planted by Sister Pauline and nurtured by Mr. Mildrew. I wondered if I could bring all my life's experiences—including the challenges—to a classroom. Maybe I could affect children in the same way that those two dedicated teachers had affected me: with hope, love, and encouragement. And so I received the necessary education and began teaching.

My first five years in special education brought much satisfaction, yet on the whole they left me feeling disheartened. I had overidealized a career as a teacher, thinking I could touch the life of every child as profoundly as my fifth-grade teacher had touched my own life. At the end of those five years, I left the teaching profession to turn my energies to other endeavors.

3

In the midst of these varied career experiences, I found myself still searching for happiness and inner peace, so I retreated from the world at a place called Gentle Wind in Kittery, Maine. Through this retreat experience, I began to be able to accept myself for who I am and to work with the personal resources available to me. It's hard to put into words the quantum leap in awareness that I was able to take.

I now continue to offer to challenged children and adults, a space (not an actual place, but an opportunity that we share in one another's presence) where we each can grow. This space is similar to the one offered me while I was on retreat at Gentle Wind. It is a space that is sacred, where each can explore, live in peace, and come to discover his or her inner self while living in this tumultuous world.

In my classroom, I hold the intention of doing my best to create this kind of gentle, open environment where everyone can learn how to learn. The Brain Gym program is the ideal resource to draw from in creating this kind of environment, for it honors the learner at any level of progress and addresses the physical comfort and ease of learning as requisite to mental performance. The simple Brain Gym activities also give me a way to address my own fears and learning blocks, thus modeling the self-actualizing behaviors I would like my students to discover in themselves.

These movements, as described in the book *Brain Gym* by Paul E. Dennison and Gail E. Dennison, are "a series of quick, fun, and energizing activities that are effective in preparing any learner for specific thinking and coordination skills ... [They are] part of a comprehensive personal development program called Educational Kinesiology (Edu-K) that brings movement and learning together in a wonderful system. Edu-K allows us to challenge any learning block and move forward toward any appropriate goal."

Having the opportunity to teach in a public school seems a perfect gift, one that offers learning experiences to me, to my students, and also to the parents of the children I teach. Just as I have been taught through the examples of others, I strive to set a good example in my own classroom. Here, I have created an ongoing workshop where children are invited to grow to their greatest personal potential. Using this intention to support a child's natural unfoldment may sound like a difficult goal to reach in a special-education setting, yet it is attainable. It is made much easier when I am able to accept myself for who I am, and when I take the time to ponder how I can best gather resources to do my own small part in making a difference in a child's life. I have learned the importance of acceptance. When I acknowledge and accept people and circumstances just as they are, I see that I have empathy for myself and others, a love of learning, and a willingness to be in the process—whatever that process may be. Then I can truly be open to the continual opportunities for learning that the children in this classroom offer me.

As I ventured into the use of Brain Gym with the multichallenged child, I was surrounded with encouraging support from my colleagues in Edu-K. At my school, the principal allows each teacher to rummage in his or her own "bag of tricks" to meet the individual challenges of each student, so I was free to pursue the use of the Brain Gym activities with my class. Because multichallenged children are very often sensorily motivated, those working with them need to promote the use of the senses (especially touch and movement), as they find ways to help the children explore their own abilities. I soon discovered that the interfacing of a child's present abilities with the Brain Gym methods creates an effective way to pursue any curriculum—while still meeting the unique needs of the child.

In my early days of interacting with severely challenged children, I discovered that journaling about my experiences was a key way to sort through all of the new and challenging learning that was occurring for me. It helped me to begin to identify what worked and what didn't work with these children, so I continued to record my experiences over the last two years. When I shared parts of my journal with a few of the people closest to me, the idea emerged that this account of my own teaching experiences could be a valuable resource for parents, family, and friends, as well as for other teachers. So it was that I began to compile my notes into a book.

My intention in writing this book is to offer inspiration. I have included descriptions of the modified Brain Gym activities that I used most often (see "Key Brain Gym Movements That Enhance Specific Developmental Skills," page 170); and yet, this is not a "how-to" book. Rather, it is a story about special children who have extensive physical, mental, and emotional needs. The setting is a public school classroom where the teacher, paraeducators, and parents are attempting to identify and address those needs through use of the Brain Gym model of education, a model that uses movement to effect whole-brain learning.

Chapter 1

Creating a Safe Environment

After eagerly awaiting my new students' arrival on the first day of school, I was surprised by the fear I felt as, one by one, the nine young children who were to comprise my class entered the room. I knew that these boys and girls (who were all between the ages of seven and thirteen) had been labeled as severely handicapped, and that they would present challenges quite different from any I had faced in my prior teaching experience. I had been told that their difficulties included deafness, blindness, autism, cerebral palsy, and Angelman's syndrome; all of the children were developmentally delayed. Yet I was still surprised by the anxiety that had been gathering within me.

Five of the children were in wheelchairs, and three wandered haphazardly around the room. The only child with any language huddled fearfully by the wall with head bowed, murmuring, "I'm thared." My first task of the day was to diaper seven children and bathroom the other two, and then there were the gastronomic feeding tubes ... My initial enthusiasm to share with these children the joys of discovery melted into deep wonderment as I thought, *Oh my goodness! What am I going to do with them?* After being away from the field of special education for eleven years, I was now entering it again at a whole new level, addressing much greater complexities. I felt as if I were starting all over again.

Throughout that first day, I was learning how to talk with a child who has no words; how to greet a child who offers no familiar outward response of facial or postural gesture; how to comfort a child who throws a tantrum at the threat of a new situation or perhaps at the discomfort of sitting in his wheelchair; how to calm a child who cowers in the corner with a scared look on her face; how to manage the behavior of a child who shrieks without any warning; and how to read the body language of a child who cannot hear or see.

Along with the logistics of addressing each child's physical needs, I found myself relearning the special-education jargon. This was important if I was going to converse with the other teachers about the most effective ways to meet the varied and extensive needs of my students. In addition, I learned the administrative details of my position: the way an Individual's Education Program (IEP) has to be developed and written, how to schedule those home visits required to ensure clear communication between parents and teacher, and how to track and document a child's progress during the school year.

In those first trying weeks, in addition to my primary focus —the children—I also needed to learn to offer guidance, direction, and supervision to the paraeducators (teacher's aides) in my classroom. I fumbled, I stumbled, and I did the best I could possibly do. At day's end when everyone had gone home, I would sit there exhausted yet still wearily working on management techniques, lessons to be taught, and the classroom schedule needed for the next day.

I pondered on my feet ... I had no time to sit down and speculate as to what would be best for the children; I simply did whatever came next and hoped and prayed I was going to be able to meet the needs of the moment.

The Children in the Circle

Each morning, as I looked around the circle of children's faces, I continued my inner questioning about how to be an effective teacher in this classroom. These young children couldn't run, play, or express themselves as could their many playground peers from the general-education classes. Yet each day I was invited to remember that what these children needed most was what all children need: playful and loving interaction with the world, so that they can discover themselves and their own unique possibilities.

As I talked quietly about the morning I had planned, I looked around at those young faces so full of the promise of today, each giving me a glimpse of an as-yet-unexplored world. Here was Rudy, speechless and curious; lively Ruthie in her wheelchair, the only child ready to start learning to read and write; Aron, often seeming lost in his world of distant silence; laughing Youana, loving to make contact through facial and gestural language; Scott with his strong, uncontrolled sounds and movements; Casey with a wide-open smile that he would flash from his wheelchair like a moment of sunshine. Here was Roni, dark hair swinging gently to a little song she hummed; Jacob, sitting quietly in his own faraway world; agile Christina, offering her strong, sometimes intimidating presence; Gaby, so quiet, content, and eager to participate. Later in the year, Lindsey, with her quick, fiery intelligence, would also take her place in the circle.

This circle of small bodies offered its own uncommon form of sound and silence, of contact and distance — its own rhythm of random movements. The individual children in the circle were, in their many ways, asking me for safety, security, and containment. I wanted to learn to answer their unspoken requests.

With all of these varied circumstances and experiences in my new classroom setting, my mind raced with ideas, but I had no time to think about how to implement them. My enthusiasm for the children was still just as bright as could be. Yet I often found myself standing before the students and wondering how to fulfill my role as a teacher: *Okay, I see the daily happenings of this classroom, and I must still ask, what do I do with all these children? How do I teach them? How do I find out what they already know, so that together we can build on it?*

Safety at the Primal Level

In the beginning, as I looked at those ten children with their intense needs, the inner turmoil I felt seemed to be communicating to me a deep desire to create a safer classroom environment. The safety I wanted for them was not just safety in the sense of fastening a seat belt when getting into a car. These children needed to feel safe at a more primal level: the body level. They needed to feel safe enough to relax, rest, and become curious about their own bodies and the world around them. I could provide opportunities for them to learn to trust their bodies and this space. I could create a mental, emotional, and physical environment that would help to address each child's particular needs while developing a feeling of cohesiveness within the group.

For me, providing a safe environment includes these six basic tenets:

1. To help a child notice when he or she feels physically safe enough to become aware of feelings, sensations, or thoughts—the prerequisite to learning.

2. To honor my own boundaries and personal space while supporting the student in learning to find his or her boundaries and personal space.

3. To "back up" developmentally by varying the Brain Gym and other movement activities based on sensory, emotional, and mental needs, including the fun factor.

4. To invite the child to participate in his or her own learning.

5. To provide structure and routine—for both the individual and the group—within which spontaneity and creativity can occur.

6. To take the time to celebrate progress, rather than moving right into the next thing to be learned.

To implement these tenets, I start by holding a loving space. Within this space exists a basic understanding that each child has his or her own limitations. Given these finite parameters, I set out to discover the capabilities within the limitations. In effect, I say to each child, *Okay, I see what you can't do. Now let's discover what you can do!* I stay in touch with my own curiosity about the child and how he learns so that he, too, can become curious about his process. Holding this loving space—which amounts to maintaining a caring observation of the child's process—seems to be the foremost component in helping a child to accept his own unique way of learning.

1. Helping a Child Notice Physical Safety

In my ongoing effort to establish a classroom where we can all learn how to learn, I constantly question how to engage the children's attention on an individual basis. I want to invite their curiosity about the unique world in which each one lives—even if that world is filled with personal struggle, confinement to a wheelchair, or an inability to control one's musculature. I want to help each child to self-identify and to find solace and levity within.

Following each of those first few days in the classroom, I began to spend one or two minutes at home imitating the behavior of each child. To whatever extent was possible, I wanted to have a personal experience of my students' individual struggles, and of what might help each of them to feel safe. So I imitated one child's particular walk; another's noises and attempted verbalizations; the constant, agitated,

11

involuntary motion of yet another. I even attempted to drool as some of the children do. I was hoping to gather information about how these behaviors might feel to each child—how they might be perceived inside his or her own body.

This imitation of specific behaviors offered great insight. I was able to imagine how it might feel to sit all day, my mouth, chin, and bib soaked with drool, my head bent over as my eyes followed the motion of a person in the room. I wondered if that child followed the motion for visual stimulation or because he wanted to say something but, without speech, was unable to—did he feel trapped in his body? I felt great awe at the undaunted joy of another child who spastically reached out for an object and yet was unable to steady her hand enough to grasp it. The frustration I felt when I imitated this behavior was immense.

This study of my students' movement patterns gave me a deeper respect for the daily challenges that they face. And, as I imitated the children's nuances of behavior, I began to attune myself to their subtle changes. I watched for a longer attention span, greater ease of movement, improved visual or motor coordination, or any increase in expressiveness.

2. Honoring Boundaries for Myself and My Students

Clear personal boundaries, in which adults feel safe to address their own mental, sensory, and emotional needs, are also essential for establishing a feeling of safety and containment for a child.

Yet, in my efforts to cope during those difficult first days, I frantically searched within myself for that sense of ease and security. The one Brain Gym movement I remembered to do was Hook-ups. Whenever I would stop, take a deep breath, put myself into this grounding posture, and say very calmly to myself, "I can do this, I want to do this, I can do this," the calm lasted only long enough for me to turn to the next task at hand. In this chaos, I wondered about the efficacy of Brain Gym. Yet I continued to do some Brain Gym activities, mostly Hook-ups, for I understood that the task at hand was enormous. The principal of the school, who was reassuringly attentive to my needs, often asked me, "Are you feeling overwhelmed?" I would always answer no, and yet in retrospect I can say quite frankly that I was so overwhelmed, I hardly knew the meaning of the word!

As each new morning came, I entered the classroom rested and with an eagerness to manage this day a little better than the one before. Yet each time I resolved to create an environment that was less chaotic, more calming than alarming, and full of discoveries for each child, I was simply left at day's end with a feeling of being out of breath. I thought, "Oh boy, here we go again." Just as I had done years before, I wondered if all of my efforts would make any difference in the lives of these children.

Hook-ups

Part 2

Part 1

13

Deep within me, I knew that I had applied for this teaching position because I wanted to share in and enhance the lives of these exceptional children. I wanted to be an adult in their lives who says to them, "Do what you can do. Find out who you can be. Grow with me." And so I humbly accepted help from the many generous paraeducators and teachers who taught me daily classroom strategies. At first my inexperience created a somewhat fragmented feeling in the classroom. Yet, as I came to see that there was never going to be enough time to do all that I needed to do, I discovered within myself a degree of acceptance. That self-acceptance provided me with a clear sense of my own limitations. I could take care of myself by staying clear about my own needs and abilities, and by setting boundaries from that place of clarity.

As I continued to create respite for myself from the chaos of the classroom through doing Hook-ups, I gradually realized that all I really needed to do was relax and do my best. Subsequently, I began to focus on simply being present with the children day to day, each moment. My own sense of personal space within this chaos began to expand as I took care of myself. I offered myself calmness, stability, consistency, and limits —an awareness of when to say no or ask others for assistance. With this willingness to be fully present in my immediate experience, I learned how to connect with each child and how to offer each the stability and consistency that he or she needed.

The turmoil I had formerly felt—both within myself and in the group dynamics of the classroom—gradually dissipated. Over a ten-week period, I gradually settled in to the day-to-day routine. Though I felt that it took me a very long time to do this, I was aware of the importance of taking this time to create a place where children could feel safe and able to exercise their natural curiosity. Eventually I knew that they now felt safe, because I now felt safe.

The idea of using boundaries to create a safe space developed gradually in my classroom, with input from several people. As one example of this input, I will share with you a story about Sigrid and Debbie that illustrates my first two tenets about safety.

Sigrid, who is my supportive paraeducator, offers much organization and loving structure to the classroom. Debbie, her assistant, models all she was taught in her years as a Down's syndrome child within this same public school system. She is now, as an adult, employed to work as a classroom aide to Sigrid and other paraeducators. When Debbie is given specific instructions and daily guidance, encouragement, and praise, she capably and joyfully fulfills her responsibilities. She has shared with me, though, what a great challenge it is to stay flexible in meeting the varied demands of the children in our classroom, and how difficult it sometimes is for her to discern her responsibilities as an aide or to make a rapid adjustment when our schedule is changed to accommodate the needs of the students.

Debbie, aide to the paraeducator in Cece's classroom
(shown here working with Roni), has discovered in her
work a sense of personal accomplishment.

One day, Sigrid taught Debbie something valuable about how to work with one of the students, a child named Christina. As impulsive as she is physically strong, Christina often runs out of the classroom and into other rooms in the building, or even into the street. Debbie has great concern about Christina's safety, and yet is often intimidated by her demeanor and behavior. On this particular day, Sigrid and Debbie had taken Christina to the bathroom, where Christina was seated on the toilet. Debbie stood about three feet from her with clenched fists, sweat on her brow, and an anxious look on her face. Sigrid saw an opportunity to demonstrate something to her aide about personal space.

As Debbie stood there, Sigrid placed her arm around Debbie's shoulders and asked her how she was feeling. Debbie answered, "I'm okay." Sigrid said that, to her, Debbie seemed a little frightened. With a nervous laugh, Debbie acknowledged that she was.

Sigrid prompted Debbie to back up about a foot and notice if she felt any different. Debbie said that she did feel better, and Sigrid said, "You see, Debbie, this is your space. It's okay for you to find a space that you feel safe in. When you feel safe, Christina will also feel safe, and she'll be more relaxed."

Sigrid noticed that Debbie's demeanor was immediately more relaxed. Wanting Debbie to notice this for herself, she prompted her to back up one more foot and notice if she felt even better. As Debbie did this, Sigrid commented to her that she noticed her hands were more relaxed now, and that she was breathing more deeply and no longer perspiring. Debbie sighed, smiled, and said, "Thank you, Sigrid. I feel better!"

Christina had continued with her bathroom rituals as this lesson about personal space was taking place. When she had finished drying her hands, everyone returned to the classroom, where Christina remained relaxed and calmly chose the next activity in which she wanted to participate.

3. Backing Up to Move Forward

In order to provide a safe, stimulating, and enjoyable learning environment, I back up to where the child is—mentally, emotionally, physically—and invite them to move forward with me. To do this I offer sensory-based activities to create an awakening in the brain so that learning can continue to naturally and joyfully unfold. The Brain Gym exercises (described on page 170) imitate developmental movements that infants naturally do on their own when their physical development occurs without stress, injury, or interruption. These simple movements help stimulate the sensory system, coordinate eyes and hands, and activate core postural muscles, supporting learning from the inside out. As the child feels safer in his own body, feels safer sitting or standing upright, feels safer and more coherent in his movement, curiosity about his body and environment naturally occurs.

As different parts of the brain are stimulated through new movement and sensory experiences, the body relaxes, the child becomes better organized to deal with gravity, and internal organization often improves. The child may begin to relate to such simple and primary internal body locations as up and down, back and front, and left and right. As increased organization of information from visual, auditory, and other sensory modalities takes place, a child may be able to learn things that no one had previously thought possible.

Brain Gym is not a panacea, by any means. Rather, it is a unique educational tool that I chose to use in my classroom, for only a few minutes a day, with the intention of creating an environment where learning begins with release of the survival reflex and a feeling of safety in the body. Learning can be a joyful, stress-free process in which small, often subtle, daily advances can add up to considerable changes in the overall abilities of the students.

As I returned to my classroom each morning, I said to myself, "Yes, the use of Brain Gym is a great idea. But how do

I get these children to move, to actually do the activities?" The magnitude of this task caused me to rethink the organization of my classroom. I knew intuitively that Brain Gym could unfold in these children some as-yet-unexperienced abilities ... but how was I going to do the movements with them? Some of the children couldn't even hold up their own hands or move their bodies in any way.

I was new to teaching children who have multiple challenges, and I knew that I needed to begin with the most simple Brain Gym activities — the ones I had learned in the introductory course. Yet how was I going to modify these activities for my students? How in the world was I going to facilitate movement with a child who cried out in great discontent when I merely touched him? The Dennisons had spent years defining and redefining the Brain Gym movements. I wanted to learn the intention of each and every movement, to maintain the integrity of each so as not to lessen its benefits. I wanted each of my students to benefit in exactly the way that he or she needed to.

I had heard the Dennisons say, "If the child is unable to do the movement herself, then you can do it for her, letting her learn from your own modeling of coordination and integration." Yet I found the task immense. The researching of ways to assist my students in doing the Brain Gym called for prolonged daily time periods of actually sitting or standing beside each spastic or rigid child, while exploring possibilities.

Further, I had no clear understanding of how these Brain Gym movements might translate into learning for my students. Yet I knew from my personal experiences with Brain Gym, and from my limited experiences of seeing the techniques used with typical children and adults, that Brain Gym can open new pathways for learning. I had no question that it should be a teaching strategy in my classroom.

I had repeatedly been advised by Dr. Paul Dennison (the creator of the Brain Gym movements and co-founder of the Educational Kinesiology Foundation) that I needed to "back up to move forward" in order to facilitate my students' greatest growth. In other words, while taking into account their individual challenges, I needed to determine each child's particular sensorimotor needs in terms of specific developmental stages.

To do this, I rely on my understanding of the growth and development of a typical child. With this understanding, I am able to gather insights as to age-appropriate activities for each of my students. By "looking back" to the infant stage of a typical child's life, I am able to glean information about patterns of movement that I see occurring among these learners. Muscle tone, coordination, sensory feedback — all of this observed information helps me to establish my teaching methods and strategies.

"Backing up to move forward," when working with multi-challenged children, means that the patterns of infancy and the first year of life that they are experiencing need to be recognized, honored, and allowed to develop through specific instruction. My previous experience in the classroom had already shown me that, if a child can be helped to feel as grounded and centered as a contented and curious infant, the delight in discovering and learning new things will unfold into a positive sense of self.

4. Inviting Children to Their Own Learning

Children have their different learning needs; I was aware that these eleven children had markedly different skills and abilities. As I watched and listened to them, I wanted to be attentive to the learning that was waiting to emerge. I thought about Scott, who was so alive, so into everything, so "all over the place," and who therefore had an unsettling effect on other children and was disruptive to the flow of the classroom schedule. *How can I assist him in discovering how to contain his own energy?* I wondered. *How might I teach such a child about personal boundaries?*

19

On the other hand, I watched Gaby and Jacob sitting quietly in their separate comfort zones, attempting no interaction with the outside world, and so accepting of their situations that they showed little motivation toward any new possibilities offered them. Gaby waited passively and very willingly for any kind of attention. Often, when she came back to the classroom from a physical therapy session, her eyes would be so lively and playful. At these times, she was very alert, attentive, and interested in the activities of her classmates. Jacob was happiest when left to "hang out" in his wheelchair or on the mat on the floor; he seemed to prefer his silent world to any ventures into classroom life. I asked myself what learning adventures I might offer Gaby and Jacob so that they would be more interested in reaching beyond what they presently experienced.

My task with Casey has been completely different. Casey's situation offers a good example of how I have learned to focus on creating a safe environment for these children through my response to them. I see his many deeply ingrained habits of movement and vocalization and have learned to listen deeply, in order to more accurately differentiate between these reflex-

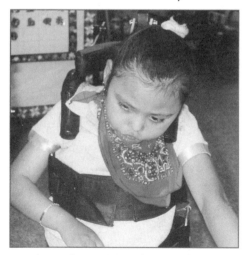

Gaby makes a delightful trilling sound with her tongue when she feels happy.

ive habits and Casey's actual communications of pain or discomfort. *Is his long, loud wail a cry for help, or only a repetitive sound made for the purpose of self-stimulation?* When I hear Casey's cry as merely a habituated response, I join him in the behavior — accepting it through playful imitation, and even creating a conversation with him

—so as to change the hue of his experience from one of isolation to one of exploration and participation. At other times, when I determine by the look on Casey's face that his cry is already a form of communication, meant to express physical need, then I respond in kind by repositioning him in the chair or otherwise attending to him until he appears to feel heard and subsequently ceases his cry.

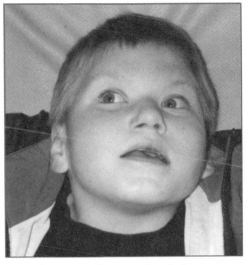

When Cece first met Jacob, he was considered to be blind. His large eyes were usually rolled back into his head, and were never observed to focus on anything.

Often, as Casey sits in his wheelchair with his hands and arms curled in rigidly against his chest, I see a certain look cross his face. Though I am not sure exactly what the expression means, I then ask yes/no questions that he might be able to answer. Casey's answers come in the form of grunts, noises, or facial expressions, and I respond in the same way I imagine a mother responds to her infant who is unable to talk. Casey cries, and I attempt to answer his needs. Sometimes he seems to be saying, "My arms and body are in knots, and my back hurts. Please get me out of this chair!" In response, I stand beside him, gradually opening his cold arms and lengthening each one, separately, to its full extension. In this way, Casey does a modified Arm Activation. This simple, one-minute Brain Gym movement nearly always brings warmth and flexibility to his arms and hands, and a big smile to his face. Casey's arms curl in again as I let go of them, but less tightly now, and his hands remain more open.

21

Arm
Activation

I have learned that, in using Brain Gym with multi-challenged children, it is very important to be patient with the seemingly tiny gains in growth that are made. And it is a comfort to see Casey being comfortable in his body, looking less tight, with his hands more open. Usually, he is then attentive and eager to partici-pate with the group. If he is not, I acknowledge him, saying, "You still don't look very happy, Casey. Do you want to get out of your chair?" If he seems relieved to hear my inviting tone, I take this as another com-munication—this time a request for more movement. I then place him on the floor so that he can experience his body in full extension, and can feel weight on his arms and shoulders as he lies prone and holds up his head to watch the classroom activities.

As I learn to create a safe learning environment, I learn to be present with the children and accept them just as they are. Perhaps they will never grow or change, yet I can find many ways to enjoy my time with them. I can listen intently to them, as though they were infants or perhaps children speak-ing to me in a foreign tongue—using unfamiliar sounds, gestures, body language, and facial expressions. I learn their language and, in that way, ask them their needs.

And I find that, as I am willing to "be in the process" with my students, I learn also to listen to my own needs. I too use the Brain Gym movements. This supports my own learning and facilitates my sense of well-being as my habits of movement become easier and more automatic. I am thus able to challenge my own learning blocks, more clearly answer the many questions I ask myself, and move steadfastly toward whatever goal I set.

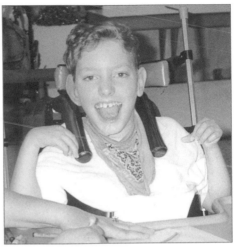

After a few minutes of Brain Gym, Casey's arms relax and his hands open.

More specifically, at the beginning of the school day I often do the Balance for Positive Attitudes, which consists of two Brain Gym activities that release tension and bring energy to the frontal lobe: Hook-ups and the Positive Points (described on pages 181 and 182). This balance gives me a moment to relax, feel my feelings, and set my intentions for the day. Also, I often select a series of Brain Gym activities at day's end, to create a feeling of centeredness and groundedness for myself, or to focus on a specific issue that I want to bring some resolution to before going home.

Positive Points

5. Using Structure to Create Safety

Children, in the process of learning and growing, continually search for ways to structure their experience. A child with special needs, who lacks the internal, body-based structure around which the average child organizes external information, needs a classroom where the structure is clear, consistent, and evident. The setting up of structure and routine is one way to create physical and time boundaries, and helps children who have special needs to experience patience, order, and intrinsic discipline. Even if a child only vaguely senses this inherent structure, the resulting freedom to learn and grow continues to expand into wonderful little miracles by the end of the school year.

During the first days in the classroom, I wondered how long it was going to take me to learn all the things I needed to learn so that I might create a structure and order that would provide the feeling of daily rhythm and consistency that I was seeking. How would I develop daily classroom strategies for knowing when to diaper, how and when to feed, what kinds of things to teach, how to set up and decorate the room for safety and interest, how to reach through the many levels of needs that these young children experience? I wanted the classroom to be an enjoyable, inviting place for them to spend the day, and yet I was aware of the possibility of making it too stimulating for those students who were seizure-prone or those who needed a quieter environment. How could I meet the dramatically unique challenges of these children as individuals and still address the needs of the group as a whole? How could I create for them a sense of comfortable belonging?

I imagined that the children sensed my inexperience; it would take time to establish the feeling of safety, stability, and consistency in the classroom environment that was my aim. One minute, I found myself running after a child who had wandered out of the room for no other reason than that the door was left open. The next minute, I would be attempting to teach a lesson to a wheelchair-bound girl when another student would grab the pencil from her hand and jeer, "Pencil, pencil!" as he ran across the room with it.

At calendar time, we would be happily singing, clapping, and doing some movement activities when suddenly a student would begin to shriek for no apparent reason. Two or three times on any given day of that first week, one particular boy would choke another boy in an attempt to hug him. The startled recipient of this affection would drop to the floor and lie there submissively like a rag doll. When the hugger was persuaded to release his hold, the boy on the floor would rock wildly back and forth, biting his hands and making high-pitched braying noises.

Within those first few days, I learned the mechanics of properly placing a child in her own wheelchair (each chair is different). I also learned how to position a child in various apparatuses used to protect the body from the detrimental effects of sitting in one position constantly: in the side lyer (to ease muscular tensions), in the prone stander (to teach weight bearing), or on the floor mat or the belly (to increase forearm and neck strength). I learned the bathroom schedule necessary to keep ten students comfortable and dry, the simple medical procedure needed to feed those children who took their meals via a gastronomic tube, and how to administer medications to a student who has frequent seizures. My skill in organizing these routine elements would provide the underlying structure within which my students could feel safe to explore.

Eventually our calendar time, during which feeding, bath-rooming, movement breaks, reading, playground time, and so on, are all included, became central to the classroom structure and sense of safety. Now, the daily schedule is exhibited on a large board at the front of the room. Key activities such as arts and crafts, bathroom time, or desk time are symbolized by tagboard icons. During the day, children come up to the board to take an icon representing their task of the moment.

They hold this icon until the task is complete, later returning it to take a new one. A structure of this kind serves as another way to provide safety and containment, and offers the security out of which spontaneity and creativity can occur.

6. Celebrating Progress

Finally, to honor the tremendous efforts that my students put forth, I celebrate each small learning that I notice. The children in my classroom work with great diligence for what many would consider small gains. I know that one of the most valuable things I can offer them is to notice, as a parent might, even the most subtle improvements in coordination, expressiveness, ease of movement, or focus of attention. Thus, I do what parents naturally do with young children: I celebrate their learning.

The celebration often gets expressed as a hug, but sometimes I give the child a sticker or a special snack. Sometimes I praise him or her individually; at other times we celebrate as a group, with the child's special accomplishment discussed or roleplayed. I like to involve the peer tutors from the general-ed campus (see Chapter Four) in these celebrations, so that they may see how their volunteer efforts are blossoming into learning for my students. Even when children with special needs are seemingly unaware of their surroundings, they do appear to absorb the feelings of others in the classroom—much as an infant senses the feelings of those around him. Thus, these celebrations have the cumulative effect of acknowledging and anchoring the new learning.

A Willingness to Be in the Process

I have come to understand that I cannot separate my own life as a learner from my life in the classroom. My appreciation of my own life experiences can only enhance the creation of a safe learning environment in the classroom. The children in the circle of my morning lesson have something to teach me, and I realize that, as a yoga teacher and Brain Gym Instructor as well as a special-education teacher, I have something unique to offer them. Through my understanding of the relationship between physical and mental skills, I am able to assess with a trained eye my students' body posture and movement. When I first met these children, many of them were clearly uncomfortable—sitting in rigid, cramped postures that put undue stress on bones, muscles, and internal organs. The absence of physical movement and sensory stimulation no doubt resulted in a lack of curiosity about the world.

Even with my trained eye, I still ask myself: *Have I the ability to provide these children with the Brain Gym activities and other sensory and movement experiences that they clearly need and lack? Can I help them to connect these experiences with the curriculum that I am charged to offer? Can I hold the belief that a few moments a day of conscious movement will produce cumulative benefits over time?*

When I thought, in those first days, of all these children and their extreme needs, I asked myself how I was going to schedule the school day so as to create a sense of ease and safety—for myself as well as for each child. How would I slow down enough to listen to the breathing and notice the body language of each child? How could I maximize the time spent with each child?

Actually, I longed to spend all my time with just one child —not because any certain one is more special than another, but because each one, individually, is so dear to me, and because slowing down is an important way to create presence and safety. Yet I realized that I have only a finite amount of time in the classroom each day, and that I must use this time to the benefit of each child, in the best way I am able to discover.

The search for answers to these and other questions is an ongoing one for me—as it is, I imagine, for any classroom teacher. This search has taught me something about the true meaning of the phrase "a willingness to be in the process."

Chapter 2

An Introduction to My Students... Who Are My Teachers

One day in the beginning of that first school year, I watched as my student Aron was being dropped off by his mother, Lauren. In that moment, I felt my heart reach out to this woman as I sensed her hesitation and her protectiveness. I felt sad. I knew that, for the first seven years of Aron's life, Lauren had tried persistently to give him experiences that would help him learn how to walk, how to talk, how to feed himself. And here she was again, dropping her son off with another stranger, holding within herself the hope that I would turn out to be someone who would lovingly teach him. I wanted to earn this mother's trust.

I wanted, too, for Aron to be able to say "I love you" and put his arms around his mother's neck, for him to be able to verbally share his world with her. Suddenly, one of those "aha" experiences of life created a new understanding within me: I realized that these feelings of sadness were my own and that they had nothing to do with what Lauren herself was feeling at that moment. In fact, months later when I broached the subject with her, Lauren said that she'd had such feelings of grief when her son was first born but had worked through the sadness, had come to appreciate his gifts, and was simply moving on in life without the overwhelming "woe is me" feelings.

I am still awed by this parent's willingness and ability to accept her child just as he is, as she continues to lovingly invite him to grow into happiness. Lauren has been able to come to the realization that Aron simply has special needs, needs different from those of the typical child. In that brief moment, Lauren's open communication allowed me to understand the true meaning of an idea so often bandied about nowadays: "Children with special needs are people too, people who need and want to be respected, nurtured, and invited to participate in life."

With this deeper understanding came a deeper determination to create a safe environment—a place of honest acknowledgment of each student's unique personality—for all of the children in my classroom. I began to address the diversity of needs presented by each child. Now, I can look back with satisfaction over the delights and challenges that these children and I have shared.

Allow me to introduce you to some of my students in greater depth, and to share a little about how each has grown during our time together. Some have accomplished small miracles during their one or two years in my classroom. In many instances, I see a direct connection between the Brain Gym activities and other sensory integration techniques that I use with them, and their remarkable and often unanticipated unfoldment.

Rudy

Rudy came into my class as an eight-year-old with dark hair, questioning brown eyes, a love of music, and a habit of exploring everything with his mouth and teeth. Rudy is ambulatory, but has no speech. Developmentally delayed due to mild cerebral palsy, Rudy finds his greatest delight in cruising around the room on foot. He has a wide stance with an awkward gait, and yet shows an unquenchable thirst to move.

29

While in my class, Rudy has learned how to maneuver the steps of the school bus so that it's no longer necessary for him to be transported to and from school in a wheelchair. After two years, he still needs physical and verbal prompting to get on and off the bus. Perhaps one day he will be able to integrate his thought patterns with his body movements in order to climb those big steps independently.

At age nine, Rudy began to comprehend simple, one-word requests when these were coupled with gestures. He continues to demonstrate this understanding by his facial expressions and his willingness to participate in a teacher-directed activity. Usually, however, Rudy's lack of coordination requires that he have one-on-one in depth assistance to accomplish a task requirement or skill requiring hand-eye coordination.

One aspect of Rudy's learning that brings a smile to my face is his new ability to comprehend cause and effect, a concept typically grasped between the ages of two and three. Now that he is ten, Rudy has begun to demonstrate his understanding of "If I do this, then that will happen." Tears came to my eyes the first time Rudy pressed the adaptive switch (a big red button) and then watched, squealing with delight, as a rocket soared on the computer screen. The establishment of this crucial foundation for future learning, and for making connections to the physical world, may one day enable Rudy to function a little more independently.

Rudy loves to move, especially to music, and he shows his delight with many smiles.

Ruthie

When I met Ruthie, she was a verbal, sociable ten-year-old who easily propelled herself, in her wheelchair, around the classroom and the entire school. Her delayed development is caused by spina bifida, and she is paralyzed from the waist down. Ruthie can carry on a simple conversation, and she enjoys listening to other people talking together. When school started, she had beginning academic skills: she could count to

Ruthie listens attentively as directions are given from across the room.

thirty and also write numbers to thirty when assisted, and she had a sight vocabulary of five words: "stop," "go," "exit," "in," and "out." Her favorite school activities were being read to, practicing her writing, and playing with cookie cutters in playdough.

During the year that Ruthie was in my classroom, she remained totally dependent on others for her personal care. She was able to feed herself, and enjoyed making simple statements such as, "Hi. How are you? What's your name?" She loved to participate in classroom activities, and often wanted to practice writing her name. With her tight-lipped smile, she kept a watchful eye on all the students, whom she very much liked to comfort. If her classmate Jacob cried, she would repeatedly say, "Why Jacob cry? I help. Why cry?"

Of all my students in that first year, Ruthie was the only one capable of holding a pencil. An Individualized Education Plan (IEP) goal set for Ruthie in September was that she would learn to recognize six words by the end of the year. By year's end, she had far surpassed that goal. Not only was she reading about twenty-five sight words, but she was able to consistently write her name with accuracy. Her mother says that Ruthie now loves to help make dinner, and will in her own way also help to set the table and wash the dishes.

Youana

Long-legged Youana, thirteen, has cerebral palsy. She spends her waking hours in a wheelchair, makes vowel sounds but speaks no articulated words, and is dependent for all her personal needs such as bathrooming and feeding. Yet she understands simple directions and is able to make choices, which she expresses by the direction of her gaze, by her facial expressions (such as a huge smile or tight lips and a furrowed brow), and sometimes by a squeeze of the hand. It is a challenge for Youana to maintain body control; that is, she flails her head, arms, and legs almost constantly. And yet she has an immensely joyful presence about her.

I soon learned that Youana's joy in life is her family and friends. When spoken to, she would pop out of her wheelchair in excitement if she didn't have her seat belt holding her down. She absolutely loves it when someone engages her in conversation, and also delights in being motored through an activity. (Motoring is a process in which someone is guided through the physical motions of a task or activity for which she has not yet developed sufficient coordination and body awareness to do the activity unassisted.)

Youana's favorite activity is to stand upright in a prone stander while two peer tutors motor her through painting, writing, or drawing. She also enjoys using the adaptive switches, which are large, colorful buttons that she touches with her hand to activate whatever they are currently connected to: music, the computer, or a prerecorded story. One of the switches enables Youana to have playful conversations with her peers. The tutors ask her certain questions, and she "answers" by touching the switch, which activates a prerecorded message.

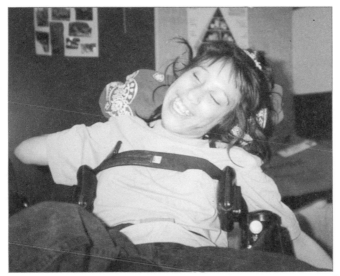

Youana responds to a greeting so happily that it seems as if she might pop out of her chair if it weren't for her seat belt!

"My name is Youana," she might announce by means of the recording, and "I am a girl." Or "Today is Monday" and "I'm going to lunch now."

Youana is delighted to now be on a full-day schedule at school. She continues to express her needs and desires by use of her eyes and facial expressions, and now understands simple sentences in both Spanish and English. Youana still needs to be diapered and fed, but is now able to go to the general-ed campus for music and art classes, which she thoroughly enjoys.

Scott

When I first met Scott, he was a charming ten-year-old who enjoyed being hugged or tickled. The plushy feel of his short-shaven hair made him a willing recipient of many head rubs, and Scott's need for tactile stimulation provided many opportunities to answer his requests for "Huggers!"

Scott arrived in class each day with a screech of delight, his bright blue eyes looking peripherally at me as he eagerly recited

33

his morning routine. His behavior was characterized by repetitive rituals, hyper-activity, and perseverance. He was diagnosed as autis-tic, yet he showed a greater propensity to interact with others than most autistic children seem to exhibit. Scott's gait was awkward, in that he would often jerk back his knee before taking the next step. His expressive

Scott loves to be outdoors, and he especially loves to swing.

vocabulary consisted of perhaps seven words. He loved being outdoors and using a swing, and he also enjoyed working large floor puzzles.

Transition from one activity to the next was extremely diffi-cult for Scott, in that he seldom wanted to stop what he was doing. My heart ached as his inner chaos would suddenly and randomly fill the room with a deafening, shrill shriek. When-ever Scott shrieked, I would do the Balance Buttons and the Space Buttons on myself to maintain my own sense of ground-edness and centeredness.

At first, Scott's outward behaviors that demanded every-one's attention just didn't match the joy that he appeared to carry in his heart. In the beginning of the school year, he would display numerous temper tantrums throughout the day, with no ability to calm himself. Without cause, he would run out the classroom door and down the hall, or out into the play yard and over to the school campus next door. Yet his heartwarming requests for hugs, together with the love of life that he revealed in quiet moments, always melted my heart and put a smile on my face.

By the middle of the school year, Scott had learned to calm himself, and the fierce tantrums no longer occurred. Following

Scott's first year in my classroom, he was able to move on to a program that emphasized simple academics.

Roni

Seven-year-old Roni, whose severe developmental delays were caused by mild cerebral palsy, was easily frightened the first year she was with me. Needing continuous prompting to move from wherever she stood, she would bow her head, wanting to be invited to play, with her eyes looking shyly up at me. Roni loves music, especially if it has a strong rhythm. Her long black hair flows in the breeze, as she delights herself by singing while she swings on the playground swing.

When I first met Roni, she used six or seven words to express herself verbally. Although her articulation of these words was distorted and she was slow in responding when spoken to, she liked to imitate what those around her said or did. However, after one year in my classroom she was talking spontaneously as well as mimicking others. Her tongue still thrusts forward as she learns to ride a tricycle. She continues to use music as a way of grasping new concepts, is no longer afraid of the rain, and spends ninety minutes of each day in a third-grade classroom. Roni's new ability to hold a pencil or crayon causes her to have a stronger focus on the tabletop activities we do in the classroom.

Roni's smile reflects her pride in her new accomplishment: the ability to hold a crayon.

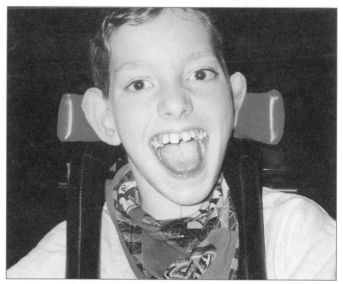

Casey often expresses delight with a wide-open smile
and loud, guttural sounds of joy.

Casey

Casey is a handsome ten-year-old boy who is confined to a wheelchair by multiple challenges that include cerebral palsy, body rigidity, low intellectual functioning, and a severe spinal scoliosis. He is unable to move at all on his own. Sometimes he seems to look at me as if to say, "I am the child who will teach you unconditional love."

Due to the absence of a swallowing reflex, Casey takes his nourishment through a gastronomic tube inserted into his belly. He drools incessantly, and is unable to use his neck muscles to hold up his head. Before we found an improved seating arrangement for him, he always had his head laid down on one shoulder. His excessive drooling causes peer tutors to regard the saliva-soaked bandanna around his neck with disgust.

Vision is Casey's strongest sensory modality, as is evidenced by the joy and ease with which he watches videos, bats at a mobile that hangs over his head, or smiles at the computer screen as he is helped to use a software program. Casey has no words, but he vocalizes often when he feels pleasure or displeasure. He will cry out when he wants to get out of his Mulholland wheelchair (one that correctly, if uncomfortably, positions his body). He will also express his delight, when getting attention from others, with a wide-open smile and loud, guttural sounds of joy.

Casey's large blue eyes are now less frequently fixed in a faraway stare. He continues to voice his displeasure when left in his wheelchair for what he considers to be too long a time, and his long, loud, spontaneous howls still express his delight when someone sings to him or when the peer tutors venture to work with him.

Aron

Aron is a happy, endearing little boy with clear green eyes and a mild personality. Although he is beginning to use words, his statements are indecipherable to most people. He makes his needs known to me mostly by walking up and staring at my face, waiting for me to determine if he is hungry or simply looking for loving attention. Aron has been diagnosed as having the neurological disease known as Angelman's syndrome.

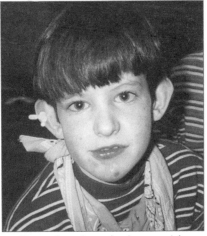

When he first came into my classroom, Aron seemed to be lost in a faraway place. Now, he often shows an urge to connect, a desire to share with others the quiet world that once only he seemed to inhabit. Although he still seems quite content to amuse himself, he also now enjoys receiving attention

Nowadays Aron looks up with delight when Cece calls his name.

from an adult. Aron's straight, dark hair is in constant motion, and it always seems a little uneven because (as his mother has said) he never holds perfectly still for a haircut. He sometimes drools copiously, and he is dependent on others for feeding and bathrooming.

At age nine, Aron now makes peripheral eye contact, and three out of five times he will come when called. He takes my hand when I extend it while asking him to come. He is becoming more aware of bathrooming skills, and is also growing more aware of those around him. During Aron's first year in my classroom, he wanted only to play by himself, but he now enjoys working with the peer tutors, and often wanders over curiously to see what other students are doing.

Jacob

When round-faced Jacob came into my classroom, he was considered deaf, legally blind, and mentally low-functioning. When I first met him, he would grunt unhappily when I touched him. He didn't want to be disturbed, as he much preferred to go on sucking his fist in his own private world. He wore a diaper, he could move from place to place only if someone pushed him in his wheelchair, he took nourishment through a gastronomic tube, he was unable to track light across his visual midfield, and he had never had the experience of bearing weight on his legs and feet. He was also unable to lift his arms or to use words to express himself, although he would grunt and moan when he experienced digestive distress.

Jacob has cerebral palsy, and is developmentally delayed to such an extent that he often sits in his wheelchair like a little old man. His immature digestive tract requires that a simple medical procedure be done for him six to eight times each day. Although small for his age, he is stout, and able to reflexively kick up his feet to relieve himself of gas or simply to move. Jacob is one of the contented, undemanding children in my classroom.

In Jacob's second year with Cece, the effects of daily visual games began to show. He now wears glasses and is able to focus.

At age ten, Jacob would curl up into a ball and make loud grunting noises, giving me the clear message: "Leave me alone!" Over time, he began to oblige me when I wanted to rub his close-shaven blond head. Eleven-year-old Jacob now stands in the prone stander for thirty-five minutes, accepts being placed on his belly while resting on his forearms for five minutes, and even enjoys being touched. Over time, Jacob began to respond to the Edu-K tracking activities that I did with him to help him learn to use both eyes together. At first he seemed oblivious of the new glasses his ophthalmologist gave him, yet after a while I noticed that his eyes could more readily track an object moving across his visual midfield. Although still considered deaf, Jacob now responds to voices more frequently, shifting his eyes in the direction of the sound, and his new glasses enable him to pay closer attention to other people or to objects placed in front of him. Jacob still enjoys time alone, so I give him "space" for this. The warmth of his gentle personality continues to invite me to be fully present with him in the here and now.

Lindsey

When ten-year-old Lindsey arrived in our class, she had recently awakened from a coma. Because of a cerebral accident (similar to a stroke in an older person), this blond, blue-eyed, bright little girl was now blind and had a great deal of sensory disorganization. Lindsey was extremely angry at her inability to speak and to otherwise express herself as she had been able to prior to the coma, and yet she showed a willful determination to regain all of her prior functioning.

Whenever I looked at Lindsey, I saw great latent potential, and I realized the necessity of accurately assessing her present developmental needs so that I could identify the next appropriate sensorimotor steps for her. She was able to feed and bathroom herself when given some assistance, but had to learn once again, as a toddler learns, to use her hands, express herself in words, find the food on her plate, or play with a friend.

Through the Brain Gym and other perceptual activities, some of Lindsey's visual ability eventually returned, as did much of

Lindsey had suffered a cerebral accident that caused complete sensory disorganization. In this picture, she was just beginning to reawaken to a comfortable sense of her own body.

her other sensory awareness. She learned to deal more effectively with her anger, and to interact in new ways. After the year she spent in my classroom, Lindsey was able to return to a general-education class. Her mother continues to do Brain Gym activities with her.

Christina

Christina, a buoyant nine-year-old, can jump a foot and a half into the air on a moment's notice. She also loves to run, climb, swim, and throw things. These kinesthetic abilities seem to be Christina's way of releasing her abundant energy. Diagnosed as autistic, Christina has a size, strength, speed, and agility that make her intimidating to both

Christine has a curious mind and is highly sensitive to other people's feelings.

adults and peer tutors who do not know her. She has an intrigue with her own bodily functions and with tastes and smells of all kinds that presents ongoing challenges to those working with her. Her single-mindedness heightens her ability to focus, yet her willfulness often prevents her from doing the many classroom activities in which she is capable of participating. Christina yearns to belong, to be a part of the group, and yet seems to ask me with her big brown eyes and beautiful smile how she might contain her own energy so that she can stay within safe, reasonable physical boundaries.

Christina is keenly sensitive to people's feelings, for she wants to be liked—especially by the adults in the classroom. She rarely chooses to engage with another child unless it is a peer tutor who is patient and kind and accepting of her rituals (such as suddenly hopping up or spinning in circles in the middle of a lesson). When she feels safe and accepted, as she does more and more nowadays, Christina will interact by listening to a story, making a papier-mâché bowl, or working a puzzle with the peer tutor. Speaking in phrases of one to three words these days, she seems constantly to be asking for structure and requesting ways to learn new things. Christina is a jubilant child whose contagious laughter brings a smile to my heart.

Gaby

Confined to a wheelchair, Gaby is unable to move her body except for random movements of her left arm and leg. A seven-

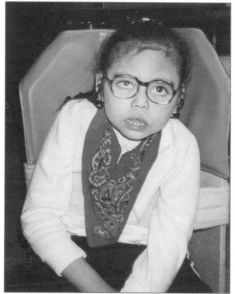

Through daily vision games, Gaby's ability to coordinate her eye movements and focus with ease has gradually improved.

year-old with long dark hair, big brown eyes, and no speech, she trills her tongue when she is happy. During her year in my classroom, I set up a way for her to play the music recorded by her father, a professional musician. She would glance lovingly in the direction of the sound whenever it was turned on. Gaby also enjoyed it when, to get her circulation flowing, I moved her limbs or did modified Brain Gym for her.

Although Gaby has cerebral palsy and is very seizure-prone, I find her eager to participate in all tactile, visual, and auditory activities done in the classroom. At the end of our year together, she still uses the delightful sound of her tongue bouncing on the roof of her mouth to express contentment. In her patient way, she has invited me into her contented world: a precious, quiet space where I can contemplate the true meaning of life and love.

Working With the Group as a Whole

My students over the past two years have had diverse basic needs that have demanded my full attention. Most wear diapers, two are drip-fed through a gastronomic tube, one has frequent seizures, three can feed themselves when given assistance, six use wheelchairs, and two thrive only in a highly structured environment. Only one student talks, with limited vocabulary and understanding. After I understood that I needed first to create a safe, fun place for these students to come to every day, I undertook to determine the needs of each child, to create a classroom where stage-appropriate learning is the goal, and to set up daily expectations for each student's individual growth.

This invitation to grow and learn has not always been met with great enthusiasm on the child's part. Often, children labeled severely handicapped are given no invitation to interact. Thus they grow accustomed to being left on the floor or in their wheelchairs, with no expectations placed upon them. This is why, when I begin moving my students (doing Brain Gym and sensory activities, testing their range of motion, etc.) and encouraging them to explore and learn—even when the learning was simply to bear weight on their feet—these opportunities were not always readily welcomed. Yet I see evidence that the children have gradually accepted my intention—I only want them to do their best. They know that I will continue to gently encourage their learning.

How do I encourage them to learn? There's no simple recipe, and yet there is a bigger picture that I shall briefly attempt to convey. It has to do with holding an intention or a goal for the child. Since few children are able to hold a goal or "feel" it for themselves, I set these goals or expectations for them. For example, I say to the child, "I would like you to be able to express your needs in words. Is this something you would like for yourself?"

Even if the child is unable to answer, he generally gets a sense that I want something for him or that I expect him to do something. The very act of asking a question invites him to explore with me, which creates a sense of empowerment. In empowering him, I believe that he will be more open to participating actively in his own learning process.

An invitation to learn is a very powerful dynamic. I have observed that the setting up of this dynamic is not common practice among most people who work with or relate to the child who has special needs. Very often we hold the idea that "This child will only be able to ..." or "This child will never be able to ..." I see it as my responsibility to continuously invite my students to learn. In creating a place where each child feels loved and safe, I have found it very important to hold in my mind this question: Who knows what this child is capable of doing or not doing? I may know what the paperwork says, but I don't know what this child is really capable of becoming.

Chapter 3

Child, Parent, Teacher: A Cooperative Learning Model

*T*he diversity of needs among a group of children who have multiple challenges causes me to constantly consider and reconsider the many realms of classroom management. I am told (and have witnessed) that the diversity of needs of just one challenged child in a family structure creates similar questions in the home setting.

At the beginning of my special-ed undertaking, when I was reflecting on what is important in this kind of education, I formulated for myself a list of questions — questions that I continue to ask as I endeavor to maintain a loving, learning atmosphere in the classroom. Nowadays, after countless conversations with parents and other teachers, I feel certain that those of us who work with special children all ask ourselves these same questions — questions about the concerns that arise as we interact with exceptional children. The tone and vocabulary of the questions may vary, but the love and the interest in the child's well-being seem always the same. The following is the list that I compiled.

■ How can I assist a child in learning to contain energy that is sometimes hyper or scattered?

■ How can I give respite from personal struggles such as those associated with being blind, or confined to a wheelchair, or unable to control one's musculature?

■ How can I help a child to manage his or her learning experience so that there can be comfort in going· beyond what has previously been experienced as a limitation?

■ How can I identify a child's ineffectual supporting habits, established out of a need for safety and survival? How can I draw out the child's intrinsic desire for growth in such a way as to release these compensatory habits?

■ How can I identify a child's key developmental needs?

■ How can I honor a child's need for the safety required to risk exploring beyond survival reflexes, so that I can invite him or her to achieve to maximum potential?

■ How can I schedule the day so as to maximize the time spent with each child?

■ How can I care for myself so that I can approach the children in a balanced state—offering a sense of centeredness and focus? I ask this because I know that, until I can be present with my own needs, it will be difficult for me to be fully present with each child.

There are support groups to assist parents in accepting their child's special needs. In my own area, the county's Special Education department offers wonderful seminars that answer some of the above questions and help parents (and teachers) meet the varied needs of the developmentally delayed child. I and other teachers like me, through our work in the classroom, add to this support.

Sometimes parents feel overwhelmed by suggestions of "what to do" from books, doctors, teachers, family members, and even other similarly challenged parents. I keep my own approach to working with parents as gentle as possible, with the simple question, "What do you want for your child today, and how can I help make it a reality?"

After many weeks of watching others on the therapy ball, Roni learns to keep her balance as she sings and bounces.

As the child's teacher, what I want is for learning to take place for my student, even though I am sometimes faced with redefining "learning" for the child who has special needs. While the dictionary defines the word "learning" as instruction; education; acquired wisdom, knowledge, or skill," I define it as reaching the greatest potential possible. For a child with special needs, "learning" may mean discovering how to stand on one's feet, learning to feed oneself, or learning to "speak" with a "yes" or "no" facial gesture.

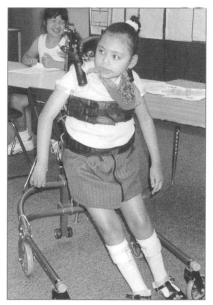

As Roni looks on, seven-year-old Gaby puts weight on her feet while supported by the gait trainer.

47

The peer tutors who come into my classroom (see Chapter Four) often ask me what I teach my students who are unable to talk or read or move under their own power. My response always centers around my own particular definition of learning. That is, rather than learning how to read, write, and do math, one of my students may be learning how to look with her eyes, listen with her ears, and demonstrate that she knows what I'm saying by performing the sometimes considerable task of moving her body.

This redefinition of "learning" is often new and different for my students' parents, as well. Many of the children in my class have been functioning in their own limited ways for most of their lives; throughout their lives thus far, their parents' highest hope for these children may have been for them to be comfortable. Then along comes a new teacher, asking the parents to consider the idea that more may be possible—even if their child has not progressed as expected, even if all hope for progress seems to have slipped away.

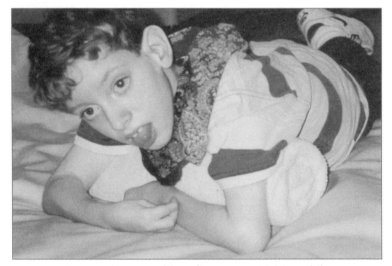

Casey enjoys watching classroom activities while doing the Energizer (lying prone over a rolled-up towel to help strengthen his upper torso).

As he peers into a mirror, Rudy is delighted
to recognize his own image.

I invite parents to be open to change, to stay alert for the smallest improvements, and, with their child, to experience an unfolding of intelligence that is measured in subtle ways. I might say to them, "Is your child more curious, more expansive, more self-contained? Does he come now when you call? Does she look at you when you talk to her?

"Remember how it is when a baby is first learning to hold a cup?" I might ask them. "He continually drops it, and instinctively we continually pick it up and put it back on the high-chair tray, knowing that, with practice, he will learn to hold the cup and eventually even drink from it." This is the patience and persistence, and the belief that learning is possible, that I ask my students' parents to find again within themselves.

One parent told me that she understood that her son was "never going to be Einstein," and yet she wanted him to be introduced to everything from which he might even possibly learn. Yes! This holding of possibilities for the child exemplifies the spirit in which teachers and parents can best work together.

Honoring the Child's New Learning

It is very important, as we invite a child to grow and learn to her greatest potential, that we be attentive to what's possible and appropriate rather than just training mindlessly. This concept has been incorporated into the entirety of this book, and is specifically presented in Chapter Five, "Ordering Developmental Priorities." When I talk with parents, I share with them that, while I love their children just as they are, I am also doing my best to provide ways for them to open to discover greater capabilities.

I invite mothers and fathers to find new ways to interact with their child who has special needs. When these parents talk about their children, I actively listen and then implement their suggestions whenever possible, for parents know their child on a different level than I do. As a teacher, I have entered a child's life for perhaps one, two, or three years. The child's parents are in his or her life from birth and for a long time to come. When the parents and I individually listen to a child's needs, and then share our observations and other information, we are better able to determine the next developmental step in his or her learning.

One of the ways that I substantiate my invitation to parents to interact with their children in a new way is by introducing the Brain Gym movements that I'll be using in the classroom. Since these movements are a series of quick, fun, and energizing activities, they are especially important for the children in my classroom, as they provide information about the body in gravity. They help the child to answer for himself such questions as: *Where is my center in gravity? Which side of me is left and which is right? Where are my eyes looking? What is top and bottom, above or below, inside or out?* Until children can experience some sense of these spaces in terms of their own physiology, it is pointless to try to teach them "up," "down," "left," or "right" for such tasks as reading or writing.

I have seen that when a child with special needs has access to the physical skills required for attentiveness (i.e., she is able to physically attend: to look with her eyes, feel with her hands, express a feeling of comfort in her body, and so on), then that child will enjoy the experience of learning. The pleasure of the Brain Gym activities is in itself a reward. The Brain Gym system offers a bridge to physical, sensory experience. It creates, for the child who has special needs as for anyone else, an easier and more joyful experience of the body.

I share with parents a way of noticing their child's growth and development. As Dennison and Dennison have written, "In Edu-K 'noticing' means paying attention to the state of our bodies and the changes, both subtle and profound, that enable us to become more comfortable, confident, and competent in our skills and abilities....When we are able to notice and attend to our experience, we become more efficient learners." In Brain Gym, this stopping to notice and then celebrate new learning is called anchoring. This anchoring, then, in itself reinforces the desire for new learning.

One of the ways that I use the Brain Gym program is to directly demonstrate to parents how the activities help their child. On our occasional Parent Nights throughout the school year, I show moms and dads how to use Brain Gym with their children. Subsequently, these parents share how they're incorporating the techniques within their children's daily lives, often as wake-up or going-to-sleep activities.

The parents describe for me how they strive to hold a space for learning and possibilities for their child. Often parents share with me that this is a new experience, and that it is exciting to interact with their child in a way that continues to invite him or her to grow. One way they do this is by being aware of their languaging and being mindful to use statements such as, "What I'd like to see is ... ," or "Learning doesn't have to be so hard; learning will get easier," or "You don't need to try; just do your best. You'll learn it when the time is right."

I am delighted to be a party to this interaction, as I feel certain that one of my teaching responsibilities is to believe in and encourage this loving space held by the parents. To me, this is what it means to work cooperatively.

When the Child With Special Needs Becomes Empowered

Since there is such a wide variety of abilities within the special-needs population, I feel it necessary to address those times when a child learns beyond anything the parent or teacher has expected: the times when a girl without sight begins to see, when a boy in a wheelchair no longer needs the chair, when an aphasic girl begins to express herself in words, when a half-grown boy who was always docile finally begins to experience "the terrible twos" and demand his independence. Although parents and teachers may see the reaching of these milestones as wonderful, the parents may also have some conflicting reactions.

Sometimes a parent has diligently worked to accept the limitations of his or her child, to come to the realization that "This is all my child is ever going to be able to do." Then the child shows unforeseen abilities, or starts saying, "No! I don't want to!" What a challenge to the parent, who must now learn to adjust.

What happens when a child's anger surfaces and she becomes less "sweet," dependent, or complacent? We teachers and parents may then come to realize that we are now dealing with the child's increased awareness of her own limitations.

Lindsey faced this challenge as she became more and more frustrated by her inability to do all the things she could do prior to her cerebral accident. She wanted to do everything herself, as she had in the past, but she was not yet capable. To add to this problem, she would become very angry at anyone around her who was encouraging her to go beyond what was comfortable.

What did Lindsey's Mom and I do? Working together, we established definite boundaries for Lindsey. These were strong boundaries, with clearly stated expectations. For example, Lindsey's mother would give her daughter two choices. If Lindsey was unwilling to choose, her Mom made the choice and Lindsey acted on that choice, with no further questions or confusion allowed. When Lindsey would kick me, I would hold her foot and say, "Feet on the floor. I don't kick you. I don't expect you to kick me. I see that you're angry. I didn't make you angry. Feet on the floor!"

It was a straight and narrow path that Lindsey trod at this stage of her recovery. Some would call these techniques "tough love." Yet Lindsey's mother and I chose to see them as effective tools in creating a space for Lindsey to grow into ... a space in which she could learn and relearn about being in her body with its new challenges and limitations. (Remarkably, Lindsey has stopped kicking, and is now able to express her needs and desires verbally and with clarity.)

It is so important to follow a child's lead. Yet what if she suddenly starts biting, hitting, or kicking, or somehow relays a message of frustration? Patience wears thin, and the bigger question of support arises. *Hmmm ... why is she kicking me? What is this child really asking of me? How can I now support a new learning? How can I be available for her, and yet not get involved in her anger?*

Seeing a Child's Needs As a Mirror

These questions become a mirror for me that reflects back to the issues I find within myself. Sometimes when Lindsey is angry, her anger stirs something deep in me. When this happens, I don't need to know exactly what it is, I simply need to let it move through me. I do this with Brain Gym—by getting into the Hook-ups posture or by doing the Earth Buttons, the Space Buttons, the Cross Crawl, or whatever I feel I need at the moment. As I do the Brain Gym activities, I feel more grounded and present with my own experience. When I create this space within myself, I can more easily transform any anger I feel about the situation, and even create an emotional container for a student's anger. This invisible kind of caring forms a palpable boundary that offers a sense of personal safety. Within this safety is a space to explore. In Lindsey's case, once these boundaries had been established she was able to find freedom within them — freedom to choose her own way of accomplishing tasks or learning her personal lessons in life. As the adults in the situation, her mother and I learned to accept Lindsey's growth and changes and to appreciate the many gifts that she could bring into our lives.

How Do We Know When to Invite New Learning?

I continuously consider these questions:

- When is teaching (whether by the classroom teacher or by the parent) intruding?

- How do I know when it is time to challenge the child and invite him to go further in his learning?

- When is it appropriate to just stop and celebrate even the smallest of changes?

- When is it important to let go of the need to teach, and simply enjoy the child's company?

- How do I stay present with each child in his or her learning and also stay centered, grounded and focused as I learn new things?

For myself, I still answer these questions with some uncertainty, yet my answers center around the notion that I must trust my intuition, trust the creative process inherent in being alive.

The following experience with my student Gaby exemplifies this idea of learning to trust intuition and the natural creative process. If you recall, Gaby is my seven-year-old student who uses a wheelchair. She has no speech, has frequent seizures, is unaware of her hands and one arm, and is essentially unable to move her own body, yet she is a happy child who knows she is much loved by her family. One day, she and I were sitting on the floor mat in the classroom. I watched Gaby reflexively swing her left arm, the right arm hanging limp at her side. I noticed that she seemed to be unaware of the midfield of her visual-kinesthetic experience.

"Gaby," I said, "I want you to learn how to rest on your forearms. I think this will help you find your arms and hands. What do *you* want?"

Although Gaby was unable to answer me verbally, I "listened" for any cues from her body that might indicate her willingness to participate in this new learning. When I determined—much as I might if interacting with an infant—that Gaby was feeling ready to expand on her experiences, I rolled her over on her tummy and placed her on her forearms. At first she stiffened slightly.

Speaking in encouraging tones, I asked her how she was doing and what she was feeling. Gaby will often show resistance by attempting to curl up her body, so, as I spoke, I used the pressure of my hand to cue her hips to stay on the mat. Softly, I told her what good work she was doing, that I knew it was

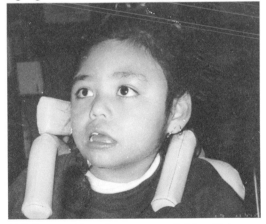

While watching classroom activities, Gaby can briefly hold up her head without support.

difficult for her to be in this position, and that I would be frightened, too (this in response to what I was sensing from her body and her sounds). "Yet," I affirmed, "it's important that you learn how to lie on your tummy."

Since that day, Gaby and I have continued to pursue this new form of learning. She is now able to watch the activities of the classroom for two or three minutes at a time, using both eyes together in her visual midfield, without distress, as she holds up her head while resting on her forearms.

Parents Express Appreciation

The parents of my students have noticed remarkable improvement in their children's development, and some have expressed their gratitude in writing. The following letters to the school principal were written by parents whose children were just completing their first year in my classroom.

Casey (in wheelchair) enjoys playground interactions with his peers.

This letter has been on my mind and in my heart for such a long time...

As you know, my son Casey has been a student at your school and is privileged to have Cecilia Freeman as his teacher. It is hard to find words to adequately tell you what an incredible teacher she is, and—most importantly—what a profound human being.

From the very first day, Cece took an interest in Casey that went far beyond her teaching skills: she became totally committed to his growth on every level. As the school year has progressed, she has remained attuned to his schooling needs, his health needs, and the needs of his spirit. She has stayed in touch with me to keep me keenly aware of his progress and problems, and has worked endlessly to find solutions for his benefit. You can imagine how this feels to me, since Casey doesn't live at home. The pain of not seeing him on a daily basis is eased and I can relax, knowing that she is there functioning from her heart. It is so comforting.

These last several months, she has implemented the Brain Gym program, with which I was familiar from Patterning in Philadelphia and from intense therapy that Casey had when we lived in New Mexico. I never dreamed that Brain Gym would be a part of Casey's school program... it is just another example of Cece's commitment to excellence!

I am absolutely realistic about my son's capabilities, and have always been pledged to maximize all that he is. Now he has a teacher who is equally responsive to those goals. I thank you for your recognition of Cecilia's gifts, as that is certainly a reflection on you—and on your school.

My heart is full of love and gratitude—not only for Casey but for all the children in his class! Their highest and best good is served from the heart.

Warmest love,
Karen

I am writing to express my complete satisfaction with my son's education this past year. Aron has made amazing progress in Cecilia Freeman's class. His attention span is up; his comprehension has expanded; he is communicating more consistently with gestures and with words (which others have finally heard); and he is also interacting with other children. With Cecilia's guidance, Aron has even worked on crafts projects, and I treasure every one of them!

Because of Cecilia's sensitive use of cutting-edge educational tools like Brain Gym, her understanding of Aron's special needs, and her excellent communication skills, Aron is doing things that people believed he would never do. I believe that he now has a chance to reach his full potential. I am not exaggerating when I say that this dedicated teacher has changed our lives in the most positive way possible. She has given us hope.

I have also seen extraordinary changes in the other kids in her class. Rudy looks like a different child, strong and healthy; Casey has practically stopped drooling; and Roni is blossoming into a smiling, beautiful little girl.

Thank you for a most incredible year. We will see you next September!

Sincerely,
Lauren

Aron's first experience on the tricycle brings a happy grin to his face.

Ten-year-old Jacob, with support from physical therapist Cindy, fearlessly bears weight on his legs for the first time.

Another parent sent this letter to the *Brain Gym Journal*:

To whom it may concern:

Please bear with me, as I never wrote a letter like this before. My son's teacher, Cece Freeman, is writing an article for your next issue. I wanted to let you know how special she is. Some of the article is about my son, Jacob. My son is eleven, and I grew to accept that I would never hear him say "Mom," feel him put his arms around my neck for a hug, or see him stand. Well, guess what? Through Brain Gym , which Cece started a year ago with Jacob, he can now bear weight on his own feet. It's a miracle. Thank you for this wonderful program, and a wonderful teacher. I just wanted you to know the joy I felt when I saw him do it. I never thought I would. What a great gift.

Thank you,
Bettina (proud mom)

P.S. The first time I saw him stand was on my birthday. It was the best gift I ever got!

Youana's mother wrote the following note to me at Christmas time:

Dear Cece,

I hope you and your family have a Merry Christmas (Feliz Navidad). To be the teacher of these children is a very special job, and I pray that God illuminates the path that you follow.

I am very grateful for the help you give my daughter, Youana. Thanks to you, she has a much greater understanding and has benefited a lot from school. She is happy that you are her teacher.

God bless you. I wish this with all my heart.

Youana's mama, Imelda

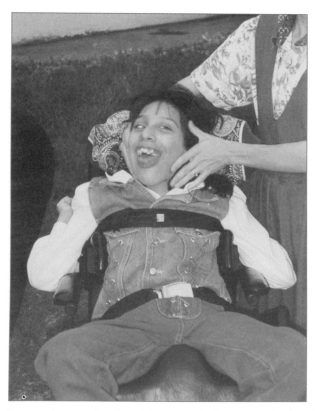

Youana loves school and homework. As her entire body exudes joy, a gentle hand stills her head for better focus.

Also, two parents honored me by nominating me for the Amgen Award for Teacher's Excellence, offered through the Amgen Foundation in Thousand Oaks, California. One of their letters follows.

Dear Committee:

I am writing this letter to nominate Cecilia Freeman for your Teacher of the Year award. Cece teaches a special-education class for seven-to-thirteen-year-olds at a school for severely handi-capped children. Her students have disabilities ranging from autism to cerebral palsy. Some walk and some are in wheelchairs. Some can feed themselves and others are fed intravenously. Some can talk, some make sounds, and others can say nothing at all. But all of them are held in love by Cece.

Conversely, these students are also teachers. Cece has told me that she silently asks each child to teach her what they need from her. Somehow, they tell her and she hears them, for Cece has had much success with her kids. Their accomplishments are testimony to this:

An autistic boy now can use words to express his feelings. Before, only his continual piercing and disturbing scream communicated his frustration. A once sullen little girl is now talkative and happy. She participates regularly with the general-ed third-graders. A ten-year-old boy, confined to a wheelchair since birth, now puts weight on his feet. Once virtually blind, he is now able to see. (This has been documented by a local well-known pediatric neurologist.) An autistic girl who used to bolt to the farthest reaches every time the door opened, now stays in the classroom willingly.

Why and how has Cece had so much success in an area where so few succeed? Perhaps the questions are a part of the key. She is always asking why and how—searching, creating, gathering, and teaching. In the process, she creates miracles. Parents and children love her for this. Please make Cece your "Teacher of the Year." She certainly is ours.

Sincerely, Lauren

Chapter 4

Inviting
General-Ed Peers

*D*uring those first few days of teaching in a classroom with children who have multiple challenges, it became clear to me that, if I was to do Brain Gym movements with my students, I would need assistance from other willing hands. For the average or gifted child, the Brain Gym activities have a simple elegance and are profoundly effective as a self-help program. However, children like Aron or Jacob might be overstimulated by touch, others such as Scott and Christina wouldn't stay still long enough to do them, and most lacked the muscle strength, coordination, or proprioception to do the movements by themselves. Clearly, to adapt the various Brain Gym processes and activities to the needs of my students would require a great deal of hands-on help.

Since the public school where I work is primarily oriented to children with severe handicaps, I went next door to seek helpers from a general-education campus that has classes ranging from kindergarten through the fifth grade. My friend and mentor at that school, a veteran teacher named Dee, suggested ways to integrate my students into the activities on the general-ed campus. She also encouraged me to find teachers willing to let their students peer-tutor in my classroom, teachers interested in fostering their students' growth by encouraging them to have caring interactions with peers who appear different. The teachers also needed to be willing to allow their students release time to help in my room on a regular basis.

A fourth-grade teacher and I developed one example of the plan for her students. These youngsters would do a modified gym class (physical education) once each week and also participate in a rotating schedule that would allow three of them to come twice a week to my classroom during calendar and music time ("circle time"). Before long, three more teachers had elected to join the program. Soon, this team of volunteering youngsters from different grade levels became one of my most valued resources. Children are natural teachers; no one can teach a child like another child. In fact, we can all learn from the open willingness that these youngsters bring to their peers who have special needs.

Ability Awareness Training for Peer Tutors

I needed a way to launch the peer-tutor program and to develop effective assistants and ongoing support from teachers. Using Dee's model, and working under her guidance, I developed my own version of a program that could be offered as a special presentation in general-ed classrooms. For this program, I retained Dee's title of "Ability Awareness Training." In this training, I talk with the youngsters about experiences that they might have in my classroom. I emphasize the following:

- A discussion about fear, anger, or other feelings that might arise from the uncommon needs of the children with whom they would be working, including the sometimes unusual appearance of children who have special needs, and about the frustrations these students may feel at being unable to walk, care for themselves, or express themselves verbally.

- An overview of "What to do if…" scenarios, to prepare students with methods and techniques to handle various situations, including practical use of special equipment.

- A discussion on the topic "What is learning, and how might children with multiple handicaps accomplish it?"

- A lesson about empathy versus sympathy, with an understanding that, when one is working with a multichallenged person, "it isn't always wonderful and it doesn't have to be."

It is essential for the general-ed students to be able to acknowledge their feelings about the appearance of students in my classroom and about what my students are able or unable to do. I also invite these students to imagine how a child with special needs might possibly feel. In the training, I speak first about feelings because, as you might imagine, it can be a very emotional experience to walk into a classroom of young children with severe disabilities. I ask questions such as, "How might you feel when you enter the room and see five students in wheelchairs, one hiding in the corner, two cruising around the room babbling to themselves, only one student able to communicate with words, and perhaps a student being fed through a gastronomic tube that's hanging from an IV pole?" I suggest that they might feel something like this: "Yikes! I had no idea these kids would look like this, or sound like this. What do I do?"

I also ask the students to consider what it might be like to work with one of my youngsters who's wearing a bandanna under her chin that's soaking wet with drool ... and she's still drooling.

"Imagine how it might feel," I then say, walking up to one of the general-ed students, if I said to you, "Oh, gross! I don't want to work with you! You have brown eyes!"

"He can't help it that his eyes are brown!" the children are quick to answer.

"That is exactly my point," I tell them. "My students can't help the way they drool. They often don't know how or when to use the muscles in their throat to swallow.

"Consider how my student, who doesn't even know that she's drooling, might feel if she receives an unkind reaction," I add. "Your response to these children, whatever it is, is okay. When you really notice your experience—what you sense and feel—and accept it, then you can feel real about working with my students, and maybe even have a good time." This acceptance of feelings is one of the most important points I make in the Ability Awareness Training, for it is essential, when these children help others, that they have an awareness of their own needs and feelings. *Then* they can be available for my students' needs.

In the practical component of the Ability Awareness Training, I explain to the peer tutors the use of the adaptive equipment (Alpha-Talkers, Able-Net switches, and computer touch windows), as well as the basics of wheelchair safety. The children are often fascinated by the unusual and innovative nature of this equipment. Once introduced to the adaptive equipment, they can bring with them to the classroom a level of capability. Familiarity with this equipment also adds to their initial feeling of comfort in such an unaccustomed environment as my classroom. In this part of the training, I use roleplay to teach the peer tutors how to work with the varied physical challenges they will encounter as they interact with my students. In doing this, I explain that this learning often occurs in "baby steps" compared to the kind of learning that they are used to. I also convey to them the expectation that I hold for the students with special needs: that, through movement and new experiences, they *are* capable of learning.

I request that the general-ed children who volunteer for the program bring with them four things to enhance the experience of being a peer tutor:

- *Understanding:* a willingness to accept themselves the way they are and to extend this acceptance to the student with whom they will be working.

- *Patience:* an ability to be calm and to persevere in the face of difficulty.

- *An ability to offer guidance:* this calls for a willingness to take an active role when working with a student whose needs are quite different from their own—a rare opportunity for most students.

- *A sense of humor:* an indispensable quality when working with challenged students, who are very sensitive to the feelings of those around them.

After I had presented the Ability Awareness Training in one fourth-grade class, the teacher asked his students to write for five minutes on how they felt about working in Cece's classroom with children who have special needs. At the end of the school year, these same fourth-graders again did a five-minute "quick write" about how it had felt to work with my students. The following are excerpts from their beginning-of-the-year responses, followed (in italic type) by what they wrote after peer-tutoring for the entire school year.

Peer Tutors Express Their Feelings

JENNIFER:

"I think that it will be fun working in Cece's room. I will also enjoy having one of her students in our class for art. I think it will be kind of scary at first, but then I will get used to it. I know Roni because she used to live by me and I have played with her and her sister. I feel good because I never have worked with the handicapped students before."

"I like to work with Cece's students and have PE with them. They make me giggle when they show they are having fun when we work with them. I like to make them giggle because I like to show them I am having a good time. I hope they enjoy working with me and I hope they are in a good mood."

WENDELL:

"I feel good because it feels good to be with them and make them happy so they feel safe with us. It might be sad but I'll try to feel what they feel. To have a good heart is important."

"Working with Cece's class is a lot of fun. I like helping them and doing things for them. I wish we could go there more."

ROBIN:

"I don't feel as comfortable working with handicapped students as some kids do. The only one I think I would feel comfortable with would be Christina, because she is a lot like me. I was very shy and was scared easily and I played by myself a lot."

"I kind of like going to Cece's room sometimes, but a lot of times I don't like it when we go there. I guess I'm just not used to working with the kids yet. Some of them are okay. I know it's not their fault they may look gross or weird or different, and some people use prejudice. I don't mean to if I do."

RANDY:

"I feel fine because I wanted to work with the handicapped kids someday."

"I feel sad for them because I wouldn't like it if I was in a wheelchair or something else. I am a bashful person like some of them. Youana and Casey, and I'm sure some of the other ones too, want more than they can say."

EDDY:

"I feel good about working in Cece's room. When I was in the second grade, I worked with handicapped kids. I think it will be good for me."

"I feel like having PE with Cece's room is a great opportunity to help me learn about the handicapped kids. I feel good and every day I am excited about the new stuff we do in her class."

COLLEEN:

"If I work in Cece's room I will feel good because I will learn some new things, like how to push a wheelchair. My mom will be proud of me because I will not be afraid to work with my handicapped cousin, whose name is Ricky. I like handicapped kids. Even if they are different, I will like them. I know how handicapped kids feel because my cousin is handicapped. I love my cousin."

"Working with Cece's class makes me feel good. It is fun to work with different people in her class. It helps me understand that handicapped kids are just like us but are in wheelchairs. I love Cece's class and I hope I get to work in her class next year. Roni is an easy person to work with, I like her."

KEVIN:

"I feel funny and weird. It might be fun but hard to work with handicapped kids and I might not like it in that class. Maybe I will like being in that class. I really look forward to helping those kids."

"I think it is fun to work with Cece's kids. I like playing sports with them, like modified baseball. I think Cece's class is fun to work with and they are nice."

JEFFREY:

"I feel like any of you would feel. People would say it's gross and they want to throw up or they feel sick. Some people think they're much different than we are, but they're not any different. They're just the same as anyone in this world."

"Working with Cece's class taught me that the handicapped people aren't so bad after all. It taught me also not to tease them because they are not any different from us. Yes, I have to admit, I do sometimes get sick of being over at her class but everything else is okay. My favorite kid is Aron. He can be stubborn but somehow I manage to get through. Sometimes I have feelings for them."

Youana (in wheelchair) and Aron (at right) welcome the opportunity offered by peer tutors to participate in general-ed activities outdoors.

SAVANNAH:

"I think that Cece is a nice girl. When we work with her students, we have to have patience. She teaches really handicapped kids."

"I feel good working with Cece's class because we are teaching the handicapped kids to do normal things like we do. They probably like to be taught by us too. They teach us a lot too."

ALLEN:

"I don't feel good working with Cece's room. I feel it stinks to work in Cece's class."

"I feel good helping them because it makes them feel good. They see people help them do stuff that they can't do. I want them to feel the same that we do when we do stuff with them. People should respect them as if they were us."

69

JESSICA:

"I think that Cece is a nice person. I'm looking forward to working with her. I once worked with handicapped kids in the first grade. They can be very nice once you get to know them. Some handicapped kids call me 'Eca.' "

"I really like to work with Cece's class because I have fun there. We do PE and sing songs. My favorite student is Roni. She is kind and funny. She calls me 'Tettida' and almost always forgets what our names are. She has long brown hair. Everyone is nice there."

JUSTIN:

"I already feel comfortable about doing it because I already know how it is. I don't think I'll be grossed out too bad."

"I feel okay working with Cece's class because her kids can be funny sometimes. I like to work with Jacob the best because he's cool. I think he is cool because he doesn't make a lot of noise. I also like to work with Youana because she is always happy. I like happy people."

KRYSTAL:

"I feel good knowing I get to help with the handicapped students. It makes me feel good whenever I help people or animals. I learned that they are just like us but don't know how to do as much as us and were just born different."

"When I go to Cece's room, I feel good afterwards. When I work with some kids, to be honest, I feel kind of grossed out. I like to work with Roni because she listens to me and she is kind of like us. I also like to work with the wheelchair people because when I work with Youana and I put her in the handicapped swing she gets really happy. She likes the feeling of the air through her hair because it's like riding in a convertible."

HILLARY:

"I think working with Cece's room is a great idea and it shows we can help others. I can't wait until Wednesday."

"I like working with Cece's class. The first time, I was excited and scared at the same time; but now I'm not. Now I know the students a lot better and I would like to work with them more. I like to work with Youana, Roni, Rudy, Casey, Christina, and Aron. PE has given me a great opportunity to see what it's like working with handicapped kids. I'm glad I can help Cece and her adult helpers. Thank you."

ADRIENNE:

"Cece's kids are probably good when you are good to them. I'm really looking forward to going over there."

"I hope that we can go more often to Cece's room because the kids are all nice. Being with them makes me feel special because some of them can't push themselves and I can help them with something they can't do for themselves."

DAVID:

"I am kind of confused about what to do and how to do it because I don't want to hurt them or hurt myself. I want to know how to play with them or walk them around. Otherwise I think it will be fun working with a handicapped class."

Ruthie (left) and Roni (right) play in the sand circle with a peer tutor.

"I think it's kind of gross because they drool and they're hard to control, but otherwise it's fun. I think it's tough work but I'm glad I'm there to help. It takes a while to get used to going there but it isn't that bad. I think it's fun."

STEWART:

"I'm sort of afraid to work with handicapped kids because they look ugly to me. I might not like it as much as some people will. I mean, something always goes wrong when it's not supposed to, like maybe someone will get hurt and it'll be my fault. I get in trouble often and I don't like to get in trouble all the time."

"I feel grossed out because they drool all the time. It smells in there too."

ERIN:

"I think it will be fun because we will learn about other kids who are different from us but the same. It sounds like I will have a great time, I hope. Cece is very nice and fun so I'm not scared to work with kids in her classroom."

"I feel good about working with Cece's class. I also feel good about being near them. It's fun to work with special education kids. Just because they are in a special class does not mean they are different from us."

LISA:

"I think it will be neat working with Cece's room because I have worked with Cece's room before because my friend Lindsey used to be in her class. I like handicapped kids but I used to be scared of them. Now I know they are nice and fun to play with and it is fun to help them learn things and teach them how to talk."

"I was a little scared, but now that I've met her class, I really enjoy working with them. I usually work with Roni or Gaby. Roni and Gaby are my favorite, well actually they all are my favorite.

Cece is nice and so are her helpers. Cece tells us what to do. We do PE and I choose a partner from my class and we then choose a handicapped student to work with."

MICAH:

"I hope I do enjoy working in Cece's room. It sounds like a lot of fun. I even might learn a lot about a handicapped person."

"I feel kind of good working in Cece's room. The kids there are fun to work with. We all do our best to cooperate with each other. All the kids in Cece's room have something extraordinary inside each and every one of them, they just haven't discovered it. I feel that even if they are in wheelchairs, they still can be my friend. They can be and do whatever they want."

JOE:

"I want to work in Cece's room. I feel sad because they can't be like us. They are nice, they are my friends."

"I feel great playing and working with them. I want to do some more work and games. When they drool on me, it feels yucky. Still, I do not mind because they are doing their best to get better. They play good games. I have fun and they have fun with us. They like us to play with them. One of them talks good. I like them."

DEVON:

"When I am in Cece's room I will say hello. I will be glad to see nine kids and I will ask, 'Who am I working with today?' But I can't make a promise.

"I feel that it is not fun. Every time I go over there I feel different because there is no one to talk to and it feels weird. We don't do PE like I know PE. Sometimes kids scare me when I'm not paying attention because they make noises and jump in their wheelchairs. I do not like kids who might get drool on me. But I do like working with them. I just feel different. I have a good time with them."

73

EMILY:

"I feel good about working in Cece's room and I do not feel scared because when I worked with the handicapped in the third grade, I was not afraid. I like working with them because some are nice. But, even if they are mean, I do not care because handicapped kids don't always know what to do or say. So I would like to help them."

"I feel good about helping in Cece's classroom because I get to help them. They are friendly with me and I don't care if they are gross to touch. If I say, 'Yeek, that is gross!' that wouldn't be nice. So I just do my best to not say, 'Yeek!' I like to help the handicapped kids. I think it's sad to say anything mean to them because they were born like that and we weren't."

LAURA:

"I feel good when I help because I'm making people happy. They would feel happy because they get help and they don't have to do it all by themselves."

"I feel okay about working in Cece's classroom because my dad is in a wheelchair. So I've been around disabled people all my life. If I'm nervous about working with a person who's not in a chair, I just pretend it's a friend I'm helping who is hurt and they can't do the things that other people can do. I'd like to work more with Cece's room so I can learn more and do more with the kids. I like them because they're nice."

Three peer tutors who came into the program late made the following comments:

NATASHA:

"I really like going to Cece's room because I have lots of friends there. At first I was scared, but now I got to know everybody. I wish we could go there more often. I feel good inside after helping in Cece's room. I like playing PE and when we play tag with balls. I like working with all of them, it is really fun. I hope we can still go there."

TODD:

"I feel very happy helping the handicapped kids and I get really excited when we go. I like going there, and usually it's fun. I feel full of kindness. I learned a lot about them and I feel sad for them. I wish to work with them some more."

CARRIE:

"Cece's room is very active and happy. I feel excited about the new song and dance we will be doing for the Spring Fling. I am happy to work with Roni. I feel glad to go to Cece's class."

I share these "quick-writes" to provide firsthand insights into the learning that peer tutors experience when they work with challenged students. The great rewards that these particular fourth-graders received as a result of participating as peer tutors in my classroom seem very clear. For many of the children, feelings of fear, intrigue, excitement, confusion, discomfort, and apprehension at the start of the school year transform into a realization that being a peer tutor is a very rewarding experience. They are able to honestly express in their writing some of the joys they experienced, some of the difficulties when they felt "grossed out" or found my students "hard to control," and the frustration they felt when finding that it often "takes a while to get used to working with them."

The personal growth achieved by these fourth-graders is tremendous: they have a great time, learn how to cooperate, are open to the opportunity of learning about themselves, and feel good about themselves as they discover how to be present for another person's needs. These young people bring courage and imagination to a very new and potentially daunting situation.

As for me, in spite of the challenges of working with sixteen additional students, I find that the benefits far outweigh the difficulties. I love working with peer tutors, love watching them make a choice that gives them "a good feeling inside." It's exciting to see them discover their ability to give joy to another child. Simply stated, it is an awesome experience for both children who have special needs and the general-ed students who participate.

A class of sixth-graders from a neighboring private school have also volunteered to work with my students. These children received their Ability Awareness Training from their teacher, Chris, who was a special-education teacher prior to teaching her present class. In her training, Chris emphasizes that the peer tutoring experience is similar to that of the ongoing buddy program at their school, in which students work with their first-grade "buddies." This prior experience in helping others, plus the fact that they're older, gives these students a special confidence when they enter my classroom.

Chris covers many of the points I include in my trainings, although her emphasis is less on feelings and more on being able to serve—i.e., to be aware of the needs of another person. This emphasis on service strongly affects the way these general-ed children interact with my students, for they seem less anxious, and therefore more able to see what is needed.

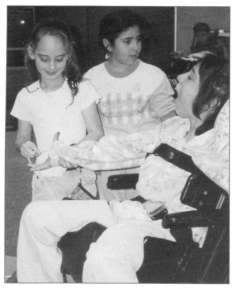

Peer tutors help Youana use a hula hoop to play "Lasso the Box"—a game that can help a child develop focus and gross-motor abilities. And, best of all, it's lots of fun!

The awareness training these students received prepared them to enter my classroom with warm hearts, open minds, and a willingness to do the hard work of helping to meet the unique needs of the children in my room. I am impressed with the ability of these volunteers to focus on the task at hand and offer guidance to my students—without a great deal of instruction from me.

For example, I sometimes give students from Chris's room such brief instructions as: "Bring the students into a semicircle, stand in front of them, and slowly turn the pages of the book, matching the words on the page to those you hear coming from the tape recorder." I can rely on Chris's students to then create the lesson. They assist in keeping each of my students interested in the storybook, calming them, redirecting those who have become distracted, or physically prompting them to stay seated in a chair. This may sound very simple, yet it can be overwhelming to bring together ten challenged students for a lesson. I have witnessed the ability of these general-ed students to create normalcy and, by their actions, express acceptance. This allows my students to feel comfortable and to also feel invited into the lesson.

These peer tutors learn to set aside their own needs in order to assist someone else to reach beyond the familiar. I applaud all peer tutors for their enthusiasm and for their willingness to be present for a challenged student's needs.

Brain Gym: Moving to Learn

With the help of the peer tutors, I have been able to consistently provide Brain Gym for each of my students, in a one-on-one experience that I couldn't otherwise offer so frequently. The Ability Awareness Training is the springboard that invites general-ed students to participate. When general-ed teachers hear about the effectiveness of the Brain Gym activities, they are often curious about using it in their own classrooms. Through teacher in-services that I present to those interested in offering Brain Gym to their own students, I am able to provide teachers with an introductory Brain Gym program. Participating peer tutors then experience in their home classrooms how and when to use Brain Gym to improve reading, writing, spelling, math, and test-taking skills. These general-ed children are especially valuable tutors, for they have already practiced the Brain Gym activities in their own classrooms, and have experienced the benefits. I can then easily teach them the particular modifications necessary for working individually with each of my students.

This year, I have been fortunate in finding two fifth-grade teachers, Pat and Coralyn, who use Brain Gym with their students and are enthusiastic in allowing them to participate in the peer-tutor program. To begin our day, two student volunteers from each classroom come to my room for a half hour each morning.

The first thing the peer tutors do when they enter my room is to quietly "put themselves in PACE." PACE is an acronym derived from the words "Positive, Active, Clear, and Energetic." The PACE process consists of four simple Brain Gym activities (described below) that allow the tutors to attend to their own level of comfort and concentration and also prepare them to give their full attention to my students. The intention of PACE is for each student to settle in to his or her own best rhythm and timing. I know that once these peer tutors are in PACE, I can count on their assistance and clarity, rather than be concerned that they will contribute to any classroom chaos or disruption.

I assign each of the four tutors to a student, which gives me and my paraeducators time to give one-on-one attention to the remaining students. After doing PACE, each tutor says hello to a designated student and, with that child, does the four components of PACE, with any necessary modifications:

Water: All electrical signals that connect the brain and the rest of the body are conducted along circuits that require the ionization supplied by the body's primary medium: water. Stress and tension are generally concomitant with dehydration. It may be necessary to skip the water with students who have difficulty swallowing, or with those who receive liquids only through a G-tube (in which case I have previously performed this simple procedure).

The Brain Buttons: For this modification, the peer tutor does the Brain Buttons for my student by placing one hand over the student's navel, then forming a wide letter "U" with the index finger and thumb of the other hand to stimulate the points under the clavicle bone. Because of body rigidity or uncontrollable muscle spasms, many of my students are simply unable to move their arms or fingers to do this exercise for them-

Youana gets help from a general-ed peer with her science homework: categorizing trees and plants.

selves. The Brain Buttons help students coordinate their vision by using the body's midline as a reference point for determining such directions and areas as left, right, up, down, back, front, inner, and outer.

The Cross Crawl: For my students who are able to move their arms or have their arms or legs moved, the peer tutor motors them through the Cross Crawl by gently lifting the student's opposite arm and leg to create a diagonal movement in a cross-motor pattern. For those students whose muscles are too rigid or spastic to allow for this kind of movement, the peer tutor simply draws a big "X" on the body, starting at the solar plexus (the center of the "X") and tracing outward with both hands simultaneously to connect opposite hip and shoulder, then repeating this to trace the other line of the "X." This activates hip and shoulder reflexes and stimulates the core postural muscles that are so crucial to establishing vestibular balance— the sense of the body's vertical position in space.

Hook-ups: For part one of this two-part activity, the peer tutor simply crosses a student's arms over his chest as though he is giving himself a big hug. Simultaneously, the tutor crosses the student's feet at the ankles. This Brain Gym posture activates vestibular balance and equilibrium and simultaneously refocuses attention on the core postural muscles. It increases one's sense of stability in space and establishes a secure center from which outward movement can more naturally originate. For the second part of this exercise, the peer tutor holds together my student's clasped hands.

As my students are assisted in an experience of PACE, I notice how their anxiety is relieved and they settle into a quiet state of relaxed anticipation. Once everyone is in PACE, the next Brain Gym movement, with all its modifications, is taught to the peer tutor. I give the tutors an opportunity to experience for themselves what it feels like to be motored through the activities, so that they can have a physical awareness and kinesthetic understanding of the reasons why they'll be doing a particular Brain Gym activity with my students. For example, if my student's learning goal is to improve her focus of attention while looking at a cut-and-paste project in front of her, I teach the peer tutor how to engage this student in simple

Roni (right) and Christina enjoy the smell of cinnamon Christmas ornaments as they roll them and cut them with a peer tutor's help.

activities related to the skill of focusing: the Owl, the Footflex, and the Arm Activation.

When these activities have been completed, the peer tutor motors the student through the assigned project. The Brain Gym activity physically prepares my student for better focus. The project then becomes a way to practice focusing attention as a new learning experience. I choose projects that are sensorily inviting as well as potentially self-esteem building, such as finger painting, making papier-mâché bowls, cutting out magazine pictures for a collage, or pasting cotton balls on a picture of Santa's beard. These are projects that my students later take home to proudly share with their families.

Sometimes, when the stimulation is too great for a student and he begins to fuss or cry, I direct the peer tutors to offer comfort, both verbally and physically by drawing Lazy 8s on his arm or leg. The Lazy 8 (the infinity symbol) is a two-sided figure with a distinct center that is especially soothing as a tactile experience. It offers a sense of balance and equilibrium as it reflects the lateral integration needed for eyes, ears, cerebral hemispheres—in fact, all neurological systems. This contact is usually enough to calm my student so that he is able to return to the project at hand. Sometimes, however, a student is simply unable to accept further stimulation. When this happens, I help the student out of the wheelchair, prone stander, or tumble-form chair, place him on the floor, and ask the peer tutor to hold his Positive Points while he lies on the mat in the classroom. These neurovascular points, located on the forehead, are very calming, as they bring energy up to the forebrain, where rational thought originates.

In this model of learning, nothing is ever forced. The student is the teacher—the leader—who communicates to the adult or the peer tutor through sound or body language what his needs are at the present moment. This is often a new concept for the peer tutors, who are accustomed to seeing the emphasis put on a finished product, and thus ask me with great concern

A peer tutor uses some gentle and affectionate physical prompting to cue Roni to focus on a classroom project.

about the reading, art, or other project they were "supposed to finish" with my student.

Sometimes peer tutors will express insecurity about their ability to comfort a student, or they may ask questions about how to attend to the feelings of a person unable to speak. These issues are covered in the Ability Awareness Training, yet it is of course a different thing to be in the midst of the experience than to talk about it. At such times, I simply remind the peer tutors that there are many different ways for people to express themselves. I ask them to look at the student's face, to "hear" her voice even if it speaks without words, and to imagine what her body movement might be communicating. Most often, the peer tutors are able to grasp this concept and to offer comfort. This interaction is really quite amazing to witness. The peer tutors develop a deep and genuine concern for my students that is wonderful to see. The feedback I receive from the general-ed teachers is that those students who work as peer tutors seem to change, over time, on a deep inner level.

Honoring Learning—for Self and Others

I vividly recall the first time I facilitated a Brain Gym balance with a group of six peer tutors, to help them reach their chosen goals. A balance is a quick and simple process that offers all the elements of an ideal learning experience. I invited these youngsters to each think of a whole-body movement that they wished they could do a little better. They became quite excited, taking turns doing cartwheels, jumping rope, bouncing a ball, and exploring other chosen activities. Then we all did a movement process together, called Dennison Laterality Repatterning (DLR).

DLR is a wonderfully simple series of activities that coordinates both sides of the body in order to teach about crossing the body's midline. This crossing of the visual-auditory-kinesthetic midline enhances brain activity and whole-body organization by simulating the natural development of the infant during the creeping and crawling stage.

After completing the DLR, each student repeated the same whole-body activity performed earlier. The tutors were amazed at the changes they felt, and at their discernable improvements in skill. They made comments such as, "Wow! This stuff is cool!" Since they had only ten minutes left before they would return to their own classrooms, I told them they had free time and could do whatever they wanted to do. To my surprise, the peer tutors all chose to line up in a corner of the room and do cartwheels, then do DLR as a group, and then line up for another round of individual cartwheels. They were all squealing with delight and appreciation as they noticed the improvements in their own and each other's performance.

When the peer tutors returned to my classroom the following day, I described goals that I had for each of my students, based on each one's skill level. For example, I stated Casey's goal as being "to learn to swallow," with the thought that this activity would give him better control of facial and neck muscles, and perhaps make him more comfortable. I also considered that, if he drooled less, his appearance might be more appealing to newcomers as he sat in his wheelchair. Together, the tutors and I then did the modifications that Casey and the other students would need in order to participate in the DLR. We practiced

83

drawing an "X" from each hip to its opposite shoulder, and I showed them how to engage vision as appropriate, in order to stimulate the autonomic nervous system for whole-body movement. The peer tutors supported my students' goals with an enthusiasm almost equal to that elicited by their own learning on the previous day.

We continue to do DLR with Casey as a daily routine. Since Casey's goal centered around swallowing, we posted an ongoing chart that indicated the lengths of time that Casey was able to swallow, and thus be drool-free. The tutors were overjoyed from that first day, when they saw the immediate results that Casey achieved with the DLR. Many days, Casey remains drool-free for as long as twenty-five minutes after completing the five-minute DLR process. The DLR is not magic, and it has never completely eliminated Casey's drooling, yet I too am amazed and delighted that such a simple series of movements can enhance Casey's ability to swallow. Perhaps, as Casey continues to experience the Brain Gym activities, the time period for which the improvement is gained will increase.

Out in the World

In addition to my students' experience with the fifth-grade peer tutors, one little girl from my class is now able to spend extra time with some of her general-ed peers. A third-grade teacher, Nancy, has agreed to integrate Roni into her class for nearly two hours every day. This is an extremely important part of Roni's day, since she is a child who expands her learning by imitating others.

If you recall, Roni had about six words (mostly fear-motivated ones) when she first arrived in my classroom two years ago. She now speaks in full sentences. Roni imitates what she hears, but can now also carry on a simple conversation by retrieving words from memory. The children in the third-grade classroom enjoy Roni, and have given her many opportunities to expand her vocabulary and sphere of knowledge. The woman who teaches these third-graders feels that Roni's presence provides immense learning for her students as well. Nancy has stated that her students are learning patience, compassion, and how to offer guidance to someone who has lesser abilities.

All in all, the peer-tutor concept offers many benefits, not only to students with special needs but to the general-ed population as well. As the participating children of both campuses begin to interact, they learn to be more accepting of their own feelings and abilities as well as those of others. In time, the peer tutors become more focused and attentive, and their noticing skills improve. They often make tremendous growth in their ability to be "present" — to feel comfortable within themselves and in their surroundings. These young people are then able to do service in the true sense of the word. That is, they are able to hold that sense of presence for special-ed students and even to have fun interacting with them. As a result, everyone enjoys the learning that is taking place.

This collaborative way of working has proved to be not only enjoyable but consistently rewarding. It has been plain for all of us teachers and parents to see that, as the general-ed peers work with the students in my classroom, the many interactions between the two groups offer to each participating child a unique, provocative, and ongoing learning situation.

Aron murmurs along with the story as a fifth-grader reads to him.

85

Chapter 5
Ordering Developmental Priorities

*I*n the first nine months of a baby's life, parents naturally recognize each small new learning they see in their child, and offer feedback to support it. They talk to their baby, smile with her, point to her nose, play with her fingers and toes, encourage her to experience different tastes, smells, and textures, and so forth. In some ways, the children in my classroom are like infants in large bodies. I clearly see that, to reach them, I have to "back up" to wherever they are developmentally. I must address their infant needs by helping each child to integrate body-related skills of visual, auditory, and motor coordination that he or she is waiting to complete or experience. This calls for my attention to the child's subtle needs and my ability to offer active and spontaneous teaching of incremental skills and behaviors. The following stories illustrate this gentle and nonintrusive process.

Aron: Discovering the World

When I first met Aron, he was eight years old and in constant motion. He walked by himself, yet used no words or actions to express his needs or desires. Aron seemed to live and move in his own little world. He did not interact with others, nor did he even seem to be aware of his own body.

With Aron, as with each of the children in my classroom, I use the Brain Gym and other sensorimotor activities to address

86

certain key skills requisite to learning how to function in the world. I derive my knowledge and understanding of these skills primarily from the Edu-K literature about brain development and its relationship to what are known in Edu-K as the three movement dimensions, which are as follows:

FOCUS: "WHERE AM I IN SPACE?"

This dimension includes:

- the experience of movement in response to stimulation of the senses, such as by light, sound, scent, or wetness

- the experience of safety within one's own body

- the experience of one's body in terms of motion through the activation of muscle proprioceptors (the "brain cells" in the muscles that help us locate our limbs and connected parts in physical space)

- the experience of relaxing and accessing appropriate musculature for resting, sitting, standing, walking, or other movement, without activating reflex behaviors

- a sense of physical boundaries

CENTERING: "WHERE AM I IN RELATION TO OTHER PEOPLE, OBJECTS, AND PLACES?"

This dimension includes:

- a sense of balance and equilibrium—the capacity to feel the body's vertical relationship to gravity

- the capacity to experience one's size and weight in space

- the capacity to feel the center of the body as a reference point for the directions *up, down, back, front, left, right, in,* or *out*

- a sense of one's own interior and an ability to contain feelings and sensations, recognizing them as one's own

- a sense of connectedness with the outer world

LATERALITY: "WHO AM I?" AND "WHAT IS IT?"

This dimension includes:

- the ability to coordinate the two sides of the body

- the ability to use both eyes together in the visual midfield

- the ability to track an object visually across the midline of the body

- the ability to match visual clues with auditory, tactile, and vestibular information

- the ability to coordinate use of the eyes and hands

- the ability to discriminate among sounds in order to internalize and process auditory information

- a curiosity about the differences among people and things

- the ability to use speech and language (both spoken and in thought) to describe needs and represent experience

Determining a child's current developmental needs allows me to support him or her in fully completing the next learning step in an organic way. Since most of the children in my classroom are continuously working on their focus and centering—their safety, spatial orientation, balance, and equilibrium—my intention is to support them first at these most primary levels of neurological development.

From my work with Edu-K and the experiences I have had with the Brain Gym activities, I know the importance of being attentive to each child's needs in terms of movement. I begin with the basic activities that enhance the child's awareness of his own weight, shape, and motion—what we might call postural and spatial awareness. Observing Aron, for example, I sensed that the first step in enabling him to develop self-awareness would be to help him feel his body and the relationship of head and limbs to his core postural muscles.

I began using the Energy Exercises to help Aron increase his sense of centering—his awareness of his own interiority as well as his connectedness to the external world. I used the Brain Buttons to stimulate his visual, horizontal orientation. The Earth Buttons could help him establish his up-and-down midline—the vertical center of his body—as a central reference for all up-and-down movements, such as sitting, squatting, standing upright, rising up on the toes, and even the more subtle movements of breathing, swallowing, and eliminating. The Space Buttons were introduced to allow Aron to experience a greater sense of motion and balance in space. And I used the Balance Buttons to help him discover the relationship of head to torso.

At first, Aron resisted any activities beyond these, as he preferred to be off by himself, providing his own sensory play with his two chosen toys. He was still quite sensitive about being touched. As the months went by, I was gradually able to introduce more Brain Gym activities. I also used my own skills at noticing to discover which of the three Edu-K postural dimensions (see the chart on page 91) was a struggle for Aron, which category of activities would most benefit him, and, when the activities had been completed, how effective the movements had been.

I did this very simply, by using a rocking motion. I would sit on the floor, with Aron seated between my outstretched legs, then slowly rock in each of three directions, one direction at a time, noticing Aron's response to each. If he had difficulty rocking with me in a particular direction, then I would do

Brain Gym movements from the corresponding movement category with him. Afterward, we would repeat the rocking, and I would note improvements, letting Aron know through my words and touch that I was pleased with whatever learning occurred.

The following chart is a tool I use to determine which category of Brain Gym activities the peer tutors or I will do with Aron. Over time, Aron began to accept any Brain Gym activity I introduced, and our time together using Brain Gym became an essential part of how we communicated. It was a thrilling moment for me when he sat on the swing in the play yard without physical prompting and imitated me by saying, "Swinging is fun!" This eight-year-old boy had progressed from wandering around in his own private world to choosing a swing to play on. Aron had actually learned to pick up his feet so he could swing. He even imitated my speech!

Whenever Aron has finished doing the Earth Buttons movement, Cece holds him, giving him a tactile experience of his body upright in gravity.

THE THREE MOVEMENT DIMENSIONS

DIMENSION	ROCK	BRAIN GYM ACTIVITIES
Focus	forward-back	Lengthening Activities
Centering	up-down	Energy Exercises
Laterality	side to side	Midline Movements

The Focus Dimension involves the ability to comprehend —to make information meaningful; it integrates the receptive back and the expressive front of the brain.

The Lengthening Activities help to release tense muscles and tendons that hold one back, making walking, running, and physical activity difficult or, conversely, leading to hyperactivity.

The Centering Dimension involves the ability to organize information between the cerebral cortex and the brainstem and between the head and the rest of the body.

The Energy Exercises reestablish the up-and-down neural pathways throughout the body, thus improving balance, coordination, and equilibrium for jumping, squatting, skipping, hopping, and related whole-body movement.

The Laterality Dimension involves the ease of communication between the left and right sides of the brain and its crossover connection to the left and right sides of the rest of the body.

The Midline Movements reestablish integrated patterns for easy two-sided (left-right) movement across the midline of the body, including movement of the hands, left-right head turning, pointing of the eyes into the left and right visual fields, and movement of the legs for walking.

This information has been derived from *Brain Gym® Teacher's Edition* by Dennison and Dennison, ©1994. For information about the specific Brain Gym movements in each category, see the section in this book entitled "Key Brain Gym Movements That Enhance Specific Developmental Skills," pages 170 to 189.

Aron's next big learning came when his mother took him to Dr. Paul Dennison for a more in-depth Edu-K balance. As a result of this single balance, Aron immediately learned to focus more attentively. He began to actually connect his vision with the toys he played with, and began to direct his constant incoherent chatter toward the toys. For the first time, Aron began to initiate brief, nonverbal conversation by making eye contact and bringing his face close to mine as if asking for a kiss. Within a few weeks of the balance, I saw Aron standing quietly next to the principal of the school as though having a conversation with him. The principal honored Aron's silent conversation by simply standing there with him, respecting Aron's intention. He later remarked to me how proud he was of Aron for being able to initiate this interaction.

Another significant shift took place for Aron in the spring of our first year together, after we began to do Dennison Laterality Repatterning daily in the classroom (see Chapter Four, pages 83–84, and page 189 for more information on DLR). As the chart on page 93 illustrates, Aron's experience was similar to those of other learners in many settings who experience DLR.

These days (a year later), I often hear Aron humming as he plays. His mother notices that he attempts to use words more often and that, most impressively, he now follows simple requests such as "Come here" or "Sit down." He now even climbs into the car after she says, "Get in the car, Aron." He responds promptly when I beckon to him from fifteen or more feet across the play yard. All of this demonstrates that Aron is no longer so absorbed in his own private world. His mother is completely delighted.

In teaching Aron, I find it extremely important to assess his abilities and his willingness to grow and learn, and then to invite him into what I understand to be his developmental priorities. My hope for Aron is that his speech will continue to become more understandable, so that he can better express his

THE EFFECTS OF DENNISON LATERALITY REPATTERNING

BEFORE DLR	AFTER DLR
Crossing the midline requires conscious effort and language brain dominance.	Crossing the midline and working in the midfield become automatic and gestalt-brain dominant.
Language brain is trying.	Language brain is choosing.
Gestalt brain is reacting.	Gestalt brain is responding.
Right and left brain may be in competitive conflict.	Right and left brain are in cooperative balance.
Learner functions without a frame of reference.	Learner functions within a frame of reference.

From *Brain Gym® Handbook,* an Edu-K course manual, ©1989.

needs and desires. As he learns to relate with people around him, it is heartwarming to see how his interest in the world outside his own mind is reinforced with every contact he makes.

Lindsey: Remembering Inborn Gifts and Potential

Sometimes a new student joins the class in the middle of the year; Lindsey, a beautiful nine-year-old girl, joined us in April. In the public school district where she had previously attended school, Lindsey had been identified as academically gifted, and had been selected to join a special program set up to enrich the education of the gifted and talented. However, in late December Lindsey was treated for severe hypertension. She then suffered a left temporal parietal infarct (a stroke), which caused her to go into a coma for nearly four weeks. When Lindsey finally emerged from the coma, she remained for some time in a semicomatose state in which she was able to do some limited motor planning—squeeze her mother's hand or open her mouth to be fed—and yet was unable to follow even simple directions.

Lindsey's hypertension had been caused by kidney failure, due to perhaps years of undiagnosed infection. Her parents had repeatedly taken her for medical exams, only to be told that Lindsey's symptoms were normal. So it was a tremendous shock to have their child, who had been about to join a program for gifted students, be suddenly unable to walk, talk, feed herself, or take care of her personal needs.

As a result of the stroke, Lindsey had no strength to get out of bed and needed a full body assist to walk. Her mother, Kim, told me, "It's as though power wires in her brain were cut in half." This complete sensory disorganization had led Lindsey to many therapists prior to her arrival in my classroom. She had received rehabilitation at a local hospital, where she was seen by occupational, recreational, physical, and speech therapists. The reports stated that Lindsey's rehabilitation centered around her sensory-input needs.

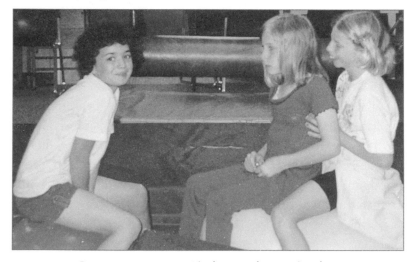

Peer tutors support Lindsey as she cautiously
learns to bounce on the therapy ball.

94

The exercises that Lindsey did during the few weeks of rehabilitation she received while in the hospital consisted of strengthening exercises such as walking with support; tongue and mouth exercises to stimulate speech; practice at listening to musical notes and imitating sounds to increase auditory functioning; playing with different materials to increase tactile sensibility; and being wrapped in blankets to enhance her receiving of proprioceptive information from the muscles.

In observing Lindsey's disorganized behavior and suppressed abilities, I could see that her primary need was to reawaken the Centering Dimension — that stable sense of her upright body in gravity that clearly had been lost due to the stroke. The story of my experience with Lindsey demonstrates some of the ways that one can use Brain Gym and Edu-K while honoring a child's limitations.

Lindsey arrived in my classroom physically fragile, experiencing immense sensory disorganization, and unable to see (labelled as cortically blind). She couldn't talk, and yet, using all the courage she could muster, she was able to walk. In cortical blindness, all of the necessary sight mechanisms in the eyes and the brain hemispheres are in place. This means that, for Lindsey, there was a chance of vision being reestablished.

After meeting Lindsey's mother, Kim, at the Individualized Education Plan (IEP) meeting and reading all of Lindsey's reports, I intuitively knew that my classroom would be an appropriate placement for Lindsey and that Brain Gym would facilitate her journey toward being the child that she could become in spite of her brain injury. Kim and I established a strong rapport. I told her that I see Brain Gym as a tool that can assist people with their learning and also as a way to return to a natural state of learning, and that I was very interested to see what progress Lindsey might make while experiencing the Brain Gym activities. Kim offered her enthusiasm and support.

I began Lindsey's daily classroom schedule with sensory activities very similar to the stimulation she had received while in rehabilitation at the hospital. I also chose to work with the developmental model of learning, in that I "backed up" to Lindsey's level of skill. I started with the one thing Lindsey felt comfortable doing and was able to accomplish independently—playing with rice—hoping to invite her to move forward with me into more advanced areas of skill and accomplishment.

I created a "rice play" center for Lindsey, filling an 18" × 36" rectangular container with dry rice and putting in a few water-play toys. This gave her an independent area in which she could explore her tactile sense, along with her sense of hearing. Lindsey enjoyed the soothing feel, sound, and scent of the rice, and I was able to begin cross-motor patterning by helping her to sift it from one hand to the other. I often sat beside Lindsey during this time and drew the X slowly across her back, tactilely connecting each shoulder to its opposite hip. Within a week, I was able to offer Lindsey a variety of other tactile and sensory feedback activities, such as dry beans to play with and wet cornstarch and playdough to manipulate.

As I observed Lindsey's attempts at movement outside of her "rice play" area, I noticed that they often appeared hesitant and labored. Her sense of body motion in space was inhibited; no doubt this was connected to her loss of vision. The excessively conscious way that she controlled her every movement strongly affected her coordination. Lindsey seemed to have lost her sense of whole-body-reflex movement, as well as the continuity of motion that is governed by the right brain, the hindbrain, and the autonomic nervous system.

Having been in a coma for a full month, Lindsey also had low muscle tone. She had great difficulty shifting from a passive to a more active use of her body, perhaps because the muscles were still weak. For example, when she was sitting, she wanted to remain sitting. Whether she was standing or sitting, she remained stationary, appearing to think and rethink her environment and to contemplate her every possible movement within it, rather than actually interacting.

I decided to offer Lindsey the Brain Gym activities and sensory experiences that might enhance her ability to stand independently or to create a smooth transition between sitting and walking. This coordinated interplay of the two elements of mobility and stability could take place only when she was able to actually experience her movements. The receptors in the skin, joints, and muscles constantly transmit information to the brain about the state of tension of the muscles, as well as about the relation of the various parts of the body to one another; this gives us our sense of posture, equilibrium, and spatial orientation. Knowing that Lindsey had previously achieved a high level of lateral integration, as demonstrated by her academic skills, I decided to first introduce the Brain Gym movement called the Cross Crawl. Dr. Dennison discovered, after researching the Doman and Delacato cross-patterning work, that the Cross Crawl activity is effective when, in Dennison's words, "it stimulates the receptive as well as the expressive hemisphere of the brain, facilitating whole-brain learning." With this information in mind, Kim and I enthusiastically offered this activity to Lindsey. We knew that, with patience, we were certain to see — at the very least — some improvement in Lindsey's relearning of her skills.

I also provided Lindsey with safe and contained areas in which to explore her newfound challenges and limitations. She was given time in the school's spacious therapy room, with large balls, balance beams, and swings, so as to strengthen her ability to move. I gave her permission, and many opportunities, to explore the classroom, so that eventually she would be able to maneuver independently within it.

Prior to her brain injury, Lindsey had been a spirited, independent child with a strong sense of personal will. I came to understand this when I spoke with some of her previous teachers, and then to personally appreciate it as I witnessed Lindsey's strong will to recover. Indeed, her recovery progressed at a rate that continuously exceeded what her doctors had believed possible. Lindsey's willfulness could be challenging when misdirected, and yet, when I did the Brain Gym activities with her, all her resistance would simply melt away. The comfort she began to feel in her own body was demonstrated by her willingness to accept the tasks that were so challenging for her.

As an example, one day Lindsey's anger and frustration at living this "new life" surfaced when I invited her to sit down for storytelling. Unable to use words to express herself, Lindsey began to resist with her whole body, while making very angry growls and grunting noises. I had planned a group activity in which everyone would listen to a story and then sing the song that went with the story. Lindsey did not want to participate in this activity, and as I repeated my request that she join the group, she backed me up against a wall, grabbed my blouse at the throat, wrung it up around my neck, and began growling at me.

One of the other students became very upset and said, "No hit teacher! Lindsey, no hit teacher!" Speaking in as soothing and casual a voice as I could find within my frightened body, I told the other student that it was okay. Lindsey was just getting some proprioceptive information, I explained (reassuring myself at the same time), and she didn't mean to hurt me. My intention was to reassure Lindsey by remaining calm and avoiding any exaggerated response to the situation.

At that moment, seven-year-old Roni returned from her integration time in the third-grade general-education classroom. As Lindsey still had me pinned to the wall, I looked in Roni's direction and asked her how her day had gone. Lindsey now surmised that her willfulness wasn't having any direct effect, and immediately stopped her aggression, letting go of my shirt and backing away.

This willfulness had been a part of Lindsey's behavior, in more subtle ways, prior to the stroke, and as she continued to get stronger, the qualities of her basic personality resurfaced more and more often. Her aggression manifested, I believe, even more strongly because of her frustration at finding previously established skills now unavailable. I saw it as my job, as her teacher, to honor her way of being, direct her growth and development, and also invite her to continue growing and learning. This example demonstrates how I acknowledged Lindsey's "mad" behavior, gently showing her that such behavior was unacceptable and redirecting her energy to a more socially appropriate way of being in the classroom.

I returned to the group and continued on with the lesson. Lindsey eventually joined us from the place on the floor where she had dropped. It seemed that she was now listening to the story, too. During our lesson, I did Lazy 8s on Lindsey's back to help her relax her eyes, neck, and shoulders. Then I stood up to do the Thinking Cap, gently unrolling the outer folds of the ears of each of the students in the circle, as I often do to help them listen more attentively to a story. As I came near Lindsey to do the Thinking Cap with her, I simultaneously did the activity for myself. I, too, needed to relax and to be able to focus, so I could continue with the group. Faced with such intense feelings and behaviors from a student, I realized again how much I value the Brain Gym system as a tool to help me quickly regain my own center and grounding. And, as I centered myself, I saw Lindsey finding her center as well.

As time passed, Lindsey gradually began to perceive a tiny window of vision. At first, this visual field was only a narrow band, directly in front of her. To facilitate the ease with which Lindsey might regain her thinking, as well as her visual and other sensory processes, I very much wanted her to experience the bilateral integration that is possible with DLR. I also had plans to do Edu-K vision training, anticipating the positive impact these processes might have in Lindsey's developmental abilities. Lindsey, however, had other ideas, and was highly resistant to such intervention. Rather than try to force Lindsey, Kim and I agreed that we needed to follow her lead. We

Lindsey, still blind in this photo, uses tactile information to paint Popsicle sticks for a Father's Day project—her first fine-motor task after her stroke.

set aside thoughts of DLR and vision training, and continued instead with the more basic Cross Crawl movement.

Lindsey continued to make strong gains with just the bilateral Cross Crawl. As we patiently followed her lead, wonderful growth occurred —sometimes from the most unlikely sources. For example, a major difficulty for Lindsey was her inability to wear shoes. There was much bemusing about Lindsey's resistance. Was it behavioral? Sensorial? We again decided to honor Lindsey's unspoken but very clear request to go at her own pace. After reading *Smart Moves: Why Learning Is Not All in Your Head* by educator and neurophysiologist Carla Hannaford, Kim began to address the "shoe dilemma" by placing socks with different textures, as well as different colors, on Lindsey's feet. Kim now recognized this as a way to offer Lindsey a structured, repetitive sensory stimulus. Often Lindsey would remove the socks halfway through the day, until she realized that, by wearing socks, she could be with her friends on the general-ed campus. This bending of school rules to allow Lindsey to wear only socks gave her the encouragement she needed to endure something on her feet for longer periods of time.

Eventually, Kim would take Lindsey for walks in the woods and randomly place piles of dirt, small sticks, or leaves in her path so Lindsey could feel the different textures. This sensory stimulation of Lindsey's feet provided a key to her further growth: as she began to look down—at her feet, at the woodsy flora, at the ground—Lindsey's visual field expanded.

Kim proved herself to be an incredibly courageous mom who believed in her daughter and constantly invited her to grow and learn and become an independently functioning child once again. Kim's openness to Lindsey's new ways of being was a great teaching for me, as was her willingness to stay present with whatever was a priority for Lindsey.

As time passed, Lindsey began to express likes and dislikes with regard to her sensory experiences, and Kim reminded her that her feet wouldn't be feeling so uncomfortable if she were wearing shoes. By June, Lindsey was wearing sandals all day long, and she progressed to shoes later that summer.

Kim and I (with some valuable input from Lindsey's psychologist) came to an agreement: Lindsey's summer needed to be spent with her peers rather than in my classroom. This would give her time to relearn more socially appropriate behaviors. By summer's end, Lindsey was once again actively participating in Girl Scouts, going on trips to the marine museum, and spending nights at her friends' houses. When the family joined a new church, Kim reported that her daughter felt accepted and included in everything. According to Kim, Lindsey was soon able to express herself comfortably amid the various church activities. Within this community, she found a feeling of welcome and safety.

The following is a summary of milestones in Lindsey's development after she left my class, starting the summer following her stroke:

■ In late July, at home with her mother, Lindsey began to see well enough to use a dry-erase board to communicate, i.e., both to give directions and to answer simple questions. This was only nine months after the stroke.

■ By September, she was using word approximations such as "peas" for please and "yeah" for yes, and repeatedly saying "MomMomMom" as one word. That month, Lindsey was mainstreamed into a general-ed classroom.

■ In October, in her general-ed fifth grade class, Lindsey began reading separate words (decoding), without much comprehension. She was not talking yet, nor was she understanding verbal cues. But on October 19, Lindsey started reading aloud, in sentences, in the classroom.

■ In late November, she started answering and following oral directions, and at the same time was offering verbalizations that were indicative of the girl she had been prior to her stroke. Initially, she was only able to follow the directive, "Lindsey, go to your room and put these away," as her mother handed her some clothes. But by Thanksgiving Day Lindsey's sense of humor was back again in full bloom. With smiling eyes, she now teases her mom with tickles and pranks.

■ After Christmas vacation, just one year after the stroke, Lindsey demonstrated that she was thinking independently. She began responding with appropriate phrases such as, "I don't want to." She also started saying, "Why can't I see more? Why doesn't my right hand work?" "Can I help with dinner?" "Are there any doughnuts?" When a "no" response came from Mom, she would vocalize her frustration like any typical fifth grader.

■ Kim told me that Lindsey's fifth-grade teacher, Pat, would sometimes cradle Lindsey's face in her hand and say, "I know you're in there, words. Come out, come out, wherever you are." This would alleviate Lindsey's frustration. With laughter, great healings happen.

With the help of her own strong will; of the expectations that I, as her teacher, had for her; and of the knowing that her mother felt in her heart, Lindsey was able to find and, to some degree, prioritize her own developmental needs. Her achievements have been truly extraordinary.

The key to working with Lindsey and her newfound challenges was to honor her development as a brain-injured child who has a great will to live and learn. The specific activities used were the sensory and sensorimotor movements, the Brain Gym movements, facial exercises taught to her by a speech therapist, and strengthening exercises such as walking, kicking a ball, running, sliding, and swinging.

Kim reports that the most effective Brain Gym activity for Lindsey continues to be the Cross Crawl. Lindsey's fifth-grade classroom teacher, Pat, and Kim still include this movement in Lindsey's daily routine. In the classroom, Pat engages all the students in the Cross Crawl, which they call "the warm-up march." At home, Kim uses it in various ways. Most often it is used passively, as when Lindsey is lying in bed and requests, "Mom, can I have my crosses?" Kim then slowly facilitates a passive Cross Crawl with Lindsey by alternately pressing the opposite hip and shoulder on the front of her body. Then Lindsey turns over, and Kim presses her body in the same way from behind.

Kim has said that on the nights that they happen to miss doing the passive Cross Crawl, Lindsey's monster nightmares and strong emotions seem to intensify. She is certain that Lindsey feels more calm and integrated when she falls asleep after she has done the Cross Crawl.

Kim continues to use the Cross Crawl to help her daughter develop proprioceptive awareness; the rhythmic, alternating, left-right motion helps Lindsey get a sense of her body in space. Prior to their daily evening walk, the entire family does the Cross Crawl together. Lindsey always begins hers by lying down, since her success rate is much greater that way than if she were to attempt to stand, balance, and cross the midline of her body all at the same time. Then, once she has gained stability, she does about one minute of standing Cross Crawl movements. Kim reports that Lindsey's "drunken sailor walk" then changes into the gait of a typical ten-year-old girl.

One day, Kim seemed to be apologizing to me for not doing more Brain Gym movements with Lindsey. I reassured her that the amount of time she was managing to give to the Brain Gym movements was certainly helping Lindsey. Children who have special needs do well with even minimal Brain Gym time in their daily schedule, if the activities are done consistently.

Kim has set a goal for Lindsey to continue to experience greater body awareness and perception of all of her senses. She has said that, if Lindsey's vision is going to remain compromised, then she would like for her to be able to fluently use all her other senses as the need arises. I'm glad that Kim keeps setting goals for Lindsey. This is an important way of ordering developmental priorities, honoring a child's need to grow and learn, and creating a focus that encourages the child to continue to delight in life—no matter what his or her challenges may be.

Chapter 6

Honoring the Child's Search for Structure

*T*here is only one way for a child to learn about spatial relationships (where things are in space), and that is through movement. A teacher can structure the classroom, organize the curriculum, make rules and set limits, and offer consistent routines, yet the child's search for structure begins with the self-organizing of his own physical body. And it is only through movement that he can create this order within his own internal system. No one in my classroom better demonstrates this idea than Casey.

Casey: "Where Am I in Space?"

Casey is always here, in his place within the circle of children. He is unlike the typical child, who has many opportunities to run, jump, climb, wrestle, and tumble, and thereby to constantly stimulate the skin, nerves, muscles, and lymphatic system through movement. Sitting all day in his wheelchair, making tense, random, and disconnected gestures, Casey seems to lack a basic sense of himself moving in his own personal, physical space. That is why, of all the children in my classroom, he best exemplifies a child's search to discover "Where am I in space?" Fortunately for Casey, early in his life his mother recognized his need for such stimulation. She began then to playfully "roughhouse" with him—something that brings him great delight, and that she also taught me to do with him. Yet, during Casey's past few years of school experience, he had mostly been sedentary. Watching Casey in his first few weeks in my classroom and noting his muscular tension and rigidity, it seemed to me that the most important learning for him would be to relax, and thereby increase his sense of his own physical body.

To help Casey with physical grounding (the sense of body stability) and thus help increase his body awareness, I selected the Brain Gym exercises that release excessive holding in the tendons. I wanted him to experience more of his size, weight, and motion in space. When I looked at Casey, what I knew about the tendon-guard reflex came to mind.

In Educational Kinesiology, the tendon-guard reflex is described as a physiological response to stop and freeze until it is safe to move forward. This postural reflex also keeps an upright body from falling. But if a person always feels as if he is in danger of falling, the tendon-guard reflex is always activated, and constant muscular tension and inflexibility is the result. When there has been injury, or when the environment is perceived as unsafe for exploration, the tendons "guard" the muscles by overriding ordinary muscular response. When the tendons are chronically tight, the muscles foreshorten and lose their flexibility. This chronic rigidity inhibits the sensations in the muscles that would otherwise provide the sense of spatial relationship and location.

This foreshortening also holds the body back behind what in Edu-K is called the participation midline—an imaginary line down the lateral (side) view of the body. When a person's musculature is accustomed to habitually holding the body back behind this imaginary line, breathing is inhibited and information from the muscle proprioceptors—the "brain cells in the muscles"—is inhibited. The sense of contact, grounding, and physical interaction is then greatly diminished.

The child's ongoing search for structure begins with a search for the structure provided by his own body moving in gravity. I believe that, for Casey as for many of the children in my classroom, movement habits have been built around an unstable sense of equilibrium. Whether aware of it or not, such children are always exerting effort to avoid the threat of falling. Thus Casey needs just the right type and amount of sensory stimulation—from touch, weight, and movement—to build his sensation of stability, of continuity, of "whereness." This helps to provide him with the sense of physical structure that he lacks.

When Casey participates, it is primarily with his voice and facial expressions; his body is held back. He is clearly uncomfortable in both vertical and horizontal positions. I wondered how Casey felt in his body—with his particular system of unyielding muscles and postural holdings—while seated in his wheelchair, lying prone (on his belly) on the floor, or lying (on his side) in the side-lyer. With the intention of supporting Casey in a new experience of internal balance and movement, I began by using some of the activities from Brain Gym, as shown specifically in the chart on page 108.

As I assisted Casey in doing these Brain Gym activities, I also encouraged him to explore his ability to make choices. I introduced him to choice making through the method known in physical therapy as eye gaze. This way of choosing is commonly offered to students who have a limited ability to move the body. The idea is that I offer Casey a choice between two objects, and he moves his eyes in the direction of the object with which he wishes to play. From the start, Casey has been able to indicate his preference only two out of five times, which is considered a random visual response. I enthusiastically began keeping a record of Casey's responses, but after two years I must report that, so far, Casey's skill level for making choices with visual gaze continues to be only two out of five times.

BRAIN GYM® ACTIVITIES USED WITH CASEY

DESCRIPTION	PURPOSE
THE BRAIN BUTTONS	
Massage of the soft-tissue points under the clavicle to the left and right of the sternum while the navel is held with the other hand	To increase alertness by releasing inhibitory visual reflexes and resetting the visual system in reference to the body's midline
THE CROSS CRAWL	
Alternate movement of arm and leg on opposite sides of the body	Simultaneous activation of both brain hemispheres
THE EARTH BUTTONS	
Holding of points on the front of the body's midline at chin and navel	To establish the frontal body midline as a central reference for directional awareness
THE BALANCE BUTTONS	
Stimulation of the occipital area while holding the navel	To increase relaxation by activating vestibular reflex points for balance and equilibrium
THE FOOTFLEX	
Holding the origin and insertion points of calf muscles while extending and flexing the foot	Lengthening of the calf muscle to release the tendon-guard reflex and increase muscle sensation
THE SPACE BUTTONS	
Simultaneous holding of points on the midline of the back of the body (at the tailbone) and the front (at the upper lip)	To establish the midline of the back of the body as a central reference for directional awareness

Month after month passed, with few apparent changes in Casey. The Brain Gym activities listed in the chart demonstrated only short-term improvements. Yet, with encouragement from the Dennisons, I continued to do these Brain Gym movements as well as the eye gaze exercise with him. I watched in frustration as Casey's increasing size and weight from his burgeoning adolescence gradually and adversely affected his posture. Casey's scoliosis grew more pronounced, and he began to cut some new teeth that were typical for a child of his age. Both of these conditions seemed to cause him greater discomfort.

I felt quite discouraged, and yet I wanted to assist this lovable boy in finding a posture that put him more at ease. Casey would look at others with such longing; his eyes spoke of his deep desire to connect. As his teacher, I often reflected on how I could help him find respite from his constant physical tension, as well as encourage him to learn new ways of expressing his unique personality.

After several months of the Brain Gym activities and eye gaze exercises, I began doing Dennison Laterality Repatterning (DLR) with Casey, as discussed in Chapter Four. I started with the goal of enabling him to gain some command of his swallowing reflex, then added the goal of helping him to feel more at ease in his body. Casey's area of greatest improvement subsequent to the DLR has been his increased presence and a new feeling of ease in his body. Before the introduction of this repatterning, he spent about a quarter of the school day lost in his own world, with little or no eye contact or apparent interest in his surroundings unless I made contact with him through firm touching, as his mother had shown me how to do. Since the DLR, Casey has become much more attentive to himself and his peers, and the frequency of his distant stare has decreased considerably.

In an attempt to elicit the swallowing reflex in Casey, I had previously used a method taught to me by Nancy, the school speech specialist. With this method, Nancy could elicit three to six swallowing reflexes from Casey within ten minutes, but I was unable to achieve the same effects. However, immediately following the DLR, Casey would stop drooling for about twenty minutes at a time. This inspired me to continue the repatterning, with the intention of lengthening Casey's drool-free periods.

After one full year of DLR, starting at the rate of three times per week and maintaining a minimum of one repatterning per month, Casey continues to be drool-free only for those twenty minutes immediately following the procedure. The rest of the time, he still drools incessantly. In the face of this frustration, I wonder what it is that Casey needs to hold his head in a position that facilitates swallowing. I go on hoping that repetition of the DLR will eventually offer him this structural stability.

Over the course of time, I have continued to do the basic Brain Gym movements with Casey. In addition to the activities previously discussed, we also do the Arm Activation (which Casey enjoys) to release tension in his neck and shoulders. I thought this tension might contribute to a lack of equilibrium in his inner ear (the feeling of falling) and thus activate his tendon-guard reflex. Because of Casey's body rigidity, I have begun "drawing" an "X" on his body by pressing on one shoulder and the opposite hip. My intention is to help him reestablish the internal postural reflex that provides a sense of physical stability and, in infancy, prepares a child to enter the crawling stage of development. I also do the

"Cowboy Casey" enjoys the class Halloween party with his friend Jacob.

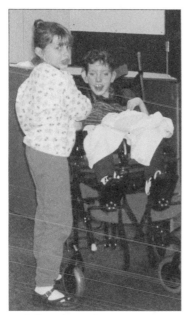

A fourth-grade peer tutor does Brain Gym with Casey.

Footflex with Casey, to release the tendon-guard reflex through the lengthening of the calf muscles and Achilles tendon, where much of the instinct to tighten originates.

Prior to doing these daily Brain Gym activities, Casey is often in distress, as one can tell by his shallow breathing and high-pitched vocalizations. I imagine he is feeling uncomfortable in his body, and so his day always begins with Brain Gym. Usually the peer tutors do some activities with him during the first hour of our classroom day. Once the initial activities are complete, Casey and a single peer tutor begin working together. Casey enjoys tabletop work. He smiles exuberantly at the peer tutor, often vocalizing the happiness he is experiencing as a result of both the attention he is receiving and the attention he is able to give to the project at hand.

However, Casey's ability to tolerate sitting in his wheelchair is limited. After about an hour of tabletop work, Casey begins to use his high-pitched vocalizations again — this time to express his desire to get out of his wheelchair. I take him first to swing on a wheelchair swing, and then he enjoys the remaining Brain Gym movements while lying on the floor. Subsequently, Casey appears completely relaxed in his body. His respiration normalizes to deep breathing, and his vocalizations often cease, except for soft, contented sounds of comfort. I can see that the tendon-guard reflex has been released, and I suspect that Casey truly feels safe and comfortable in his body and is able to be more attentive to his surroundings during these brief periods. He now rests prone on his forearms for about twenty minutes at a time as he watches life in the classroom.

Maintaining Consistent Expectations: Rudy

When Rudy is playing independently, he will pick up an object, immediately place it in his mouth, and begin to chew it and tear it with his teeth. Rudy is indiscriminate about what goes in his mouth. When I take an object from him, saying, "Rudy needs to look at this, no eat," he expresses his discontent by making a grunting, squeaking noise as he rocks forward and back.

At first, Rudy had great difficulty focusing on anything other than food. Characteristically, he would spend his time rocking back and forth in a state of apparent anxiety. Since lymph is pumped through the body by means of muscle contractions, I interpreted this motion as indicating a need for lymphatic stimulation. When I touched Rudy's back, I could feel that the tendons there (the fibers that attach the muscle to the bone) were quite tense and taut. Knowing that such tight muscles and tendons would generally inhibit an easy flow of arterial and lymphatic circulation, I wanted to offer Rudy a way to lengthen these fibers.

I began using the Brain Gym Lengthening Activities with Rudy—especially the Footflex, to release the Achilles tendons; the Calf Pump, to release the backs of the calf muscles; and the Receptive Owl, to relax the upper trapezius muscles for easier head turning. As his muscles and tendons are lengthened, Rudy becomes more relaxed. Each time Rudy relaxes these muscles and tendons, I see an immediate increase in his ability to focus. The increased focus provides Rudy with opportunities to reach beyond the familiar act of chewing everything he picks up. He continues to enjoy these Brain Gym activities.

Rudy also enjoys hearing simple songs, so whenever we do the movements together, I sing a song to him. The song is usually spontaneously created. For example, as I rock Rudy back and forth with the Rocker movement, I might sing, "Rock-a-bye Rudy, on the class floor. He rocks and he rocks, 'cause he likes some more." Then I might take his foot to begin the Footflex as I continue to sing, "Rock-a-bye Rudy, with his big foot. He moves back and forth, 'cause he likes his foot."

Since his introduction to Brain Gym, Rudy listens and focuses more attentively.

Right from the start, I saw how these silly songs calm Rudy. His face lights up, a big smile appears, and his large brown eyes sparkle as he tilts his head to the left in an apparent effort to hear more clearly. The singing seems to help him to accept the movements, so that I am more readily able to engage him in them. I also take this opportunity to bring in the skill of naming body parts as I sing and move these parts on Rudy's own body. Because Rudy has no expressive language skills, the extent of his receptive language skills is unknown to me. I have no sure way to determine what makes sense to him or how much he understands. So I consistently and repeatedly give him reminders or "prompts" of whatever he is learning. For instance, at various times in the school day, I will tap on Rudy's feet as he stands still and say, "Rudy is standing on his feet on the floor. Rudy … feet … floor." A prompt of this kind is given randomly throughout the day, based on the morning's lesson, which always begins with the naming of a specific body part.

In addition to using the Brain Gym movements to enhance Rudy's ability to focus, relax, and be aware of his own body parts, I also use the verbal and physical prompts to increase his awareness of his own behaviors. I noticed that, during lunch-time, Rudy was constantly up and down, in a continuous search for food. He simply wasn't attending to the food in front of him. He would take a bite, then drop the sandwich or apple and reflexively push back his chair to get up and go look for something else to eat, not realizing that he'd just dropped his food on the table or floor. I wanted Rudy to have a stronger awareness of his own body sitting at the table, feet on the floor, and for him to be able to improve his focus on what was in front of him.

Rudy would come to the lunch table only when verbally and physically prompted. Then Sigrid started coaxing him to the table without the physical prompts by saying, "Rudy, it's time for lunch. Come to the lunch table." Rudy would look up and twist his head to the left as if he were processing what was being said, but he seldom would move from the place he stood or sat.

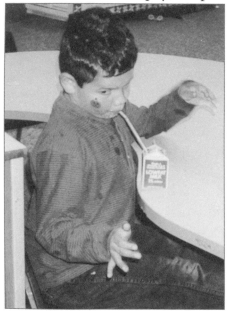

In the middle of a classroom Halloween party, Rudy discovers for the first time how to drink from a straw.

Sigrid then started coupling the same words with a plateful of food briefly passed in front of his face, so that he could smell the food. As she put the plate on the table, she said, "Rudy, here's your food. Do you want to eat?" It took many repetitions of this sequence of behavior

114

shaping, over a period of perhaps three weeks, but since then Rudy has been responding to spoken prompts by going to the table at lunchtime in search of food. He still needs physical prompting to be seated, but Rudy's attentiveness and ability to focus have greatly increased. I suspect that there has been a carry-over or a generalization made from the Brain Gym movements he has experienced as part of his morning routine.

The learning that has taken place regarding Rudy's ability to respond to a verbal request has been phenomenal. Rudy now sits at the table for twenty minutes with minimal physical prompts, and when music is played during lunchtime he appears to be more relaxed.

An important point is that the changes in Rudy's behavior have been consistent even on the many days that, due to our busy schedule, Brain Gym has not been an extensive part of his routine. Apparently, even minimal use of the movements can create learning that supports continued natural development, if we allow for it. In fact, research done on Brain Gym and new learning suggests that the movements strengthen neural functioning in the brain, even if they are done inconsistently. In any event, I'm very pleased to be able to say that Rudy is now more relaxed, focused, and at ease when he's eating.

Chapter 7

Establishing Boundaries

*U*sually when a child hits, pushes, bites, or otherwise intrudes on other people's boundaries, she is communicating that she does not herself feel safe. A child who is out of control needs to know that someone will love her enough to protect her from harm—and that includes keeping her safe from hurting others.

Creating Safety and Containment: Christina

After nearly eight weeks in my classroom, Christina still spent most of the day crouched in the corner looking around fearfully, or running suddenly out of the classroom for no apparent reason. She did not trust me as her teacher, did not trust Sigrid, my paraeducator, did not use words to ask for what she needed, was not able to wait for something she wanted, and seemed to be so sensitive to the emotive quality of the adults in her world that she took most of her behavioral cues from any subtle feeling tones that they expressed.

Because she was large for her age, strong, and quick to respond, Christina exerted an influence in the classroom that peer tutors and paraeducators alike sometimes found formidable. She seemed unable to contain her energy, often throwing objects or knocking things over without noticing, and frequently

116

creating a disruption in the classroom. For this reason, Christina needed to be constantly reassured that she could be kept safe, not only safe from being hurt or from hurting herself, but safe from disrupting the order of the classroom. We emphasized her sense of safety by offering a consistent routine, structure, and containment of her need to "act out."

One day, when it was time for lunch, eight-year-old Christina ran to get the thermal bag she had brought from home. She quickly assessed that she didn't care for what was in her lunch bag; instead, she wanted a muffin from the school lunch tray. Sigrid told her she could have a muffin after she ate her own lunch. However, while Sigrid was readying the remaining students in the classroom to begin eating, Christina made repeated attempts to sneak a muffin. The ever-patient Sigrid, attentive to potential crisis as well as to a teachable moment, gestured to me that she needed to deal with this situation rather than to participate in feeding the other children, and I nodded affirmatively.

Sigrid sat down next to Christina. She placed a muffin on a paper plate right in front of herself on the table, her arms around the plate to protect the muffin. She said to Christina, "What does Christina want? Christina want muffin?" The child quickly answered, "Christina want muffin!"

"Christina's lunch first, then muffin," Sigrid said matter-of-factly, pointing to each.

Christina replied, "Christina no want!" as she pushed her own lunch away. Sigrid said, "I see you want some muffin. Sandwich first, then muffin."

Christina made a grab for the muffin. Sigrid enclosed it even more protectively and said, "Sigrid's muffin. Christina eat sandwich first, then she can have some of Sigrid's muffin."

Christina pushed away her sandwich and said, "Christina want muffin."

Sigrid repeated, "Sigrid's muffin. Christina eat some of her lunch first, then she can have some of my muffin."

By now, Christina was clearly very angry and frustrated. She hurled her lunch bag, and each item in it, across the room, yelling, "Christina no want!"

Sigrid calmly picked up the juice box, the sandwich, and the lunch bag, placed them in front of Christina, and stated again, "Christina eat some of her lunch, then she can have some of Sigrid's muffin."

Christina began to cry with frustration. Sigrid simply sat there beside her. After about thirty seconds, she asked Christina if she wanted a drink and offered her the juice box. Christina took a sip, and Sigrid said, "Good, Christina. You ate some of your lunch! Now you get some of my muffin."

Christina snatched the piece of muffin off the paper plate that Sigrid had placed in front of her, checked it with a sniff as if to confirm that it was real, and quickly ate it.

Sigrid again stated, "Christina eat some of her lunch. Sigrid give some of her muffin."

Christina seemingly understood that Sigrid meant what she said, for she took another sip of her juice, and received another piece of muffin. Then she began to cry. The conflict had ended.

Sigrid said, "That's right—Christina earned muffin! Christina want drink?" Christina motioned to Sigrid that she no longer wanted the muffin nor anything more to drink. The consistency and structure had made her feel safe and contained, and now she simply wanted Sigrid's approval and warm attention. Christina asked for this kind of attention by placing Sigrid's arm around her back and snuggling up next to her, as Sigrid remained in the chair beside her. Sigrid told Christina that she needed to help feed the other children in the room, and asked Christina if she would like to help her. Christina gestured yes, and together they rose to gather the food for another student.

It truly is amazing to watch this kind of conscious interaction in the classroom. Even though it was extremely difficult, Christina responded favorably to the structure that was imposed for her. Sigrid facilitated Christina's lesson about the containment of needs by re-maining calm, patient, persis-tent, and ever-vigilant about the language she used with her. She clearly communicated that she was going to hold the in-tention for Christina to listen and to follow directions, until the child responded. This served as an effective demonstration of one way to establish structure and containment.

So often, children like Chris-tina need only to be shown where the limits are and what is expected of them within those limits. Then they are able to more easily participate

To assist her in discovering her boundaries and focusing on some table work, Sigrid physically contains Christina.

in classroom activities. Christina longs to be part of the group dynamic. Yet, because of her difficulty in establishing and maintaining her own sense of personal safety, she often gets frustrated. Therefore, the adults in her world need to establish a safe structure for her, with the intention that she will some-day discover her own internal structure.

Territories and the Sense of Smell

Christina thoroughly enjoys her sense of smell. She smells everything, and often will want to eat what she has sniffed. My first thought when I saw her smelling an unused diaper in the supply corner was to substitute something else for the diaper. But Sigrid wisely said, "She obviously needs to smell things." Educator and Brain Gym founder Paul Dennison later con-firmed that we needed to honor Christina's smelling wishes, pointing out that use of the sense of smell helps to integrate the midbrain, and reminding me that animals use that sense to identify their territories. Christina was probably using smell instinctively, to search for her safe space and to "ground" herself.

So Christina's mother and I put together a "smelling basket" filled with articles such as potpourri or eucalyptus cream, or with cotton balls scented with Dad's cologne, Mom's perfume, lemon juice, or shaving cream. Each day, upon Christina's arrival at school, we take her to a quiet corner in the classroom where she can use all the scents from the basket for her settling-down process. When Christina is grounded in this way, she is more present and seems to be more aware of her body. She is quieter and more centered, and therefore less apt to run aimlessly around the room, looking for things of interest, or to otherwise engage in disruptive behavior.

Ever since Sigrid and I noticed the grounding that occurs for Christina when her sense of smell is stimulated, we have taken to directing her to the smelling basket at any time when it seems she may need help in settling down. Also, while Christina's attention is engaged by the smelling basket, I often guide her in some Lengthening Activities from Brain Gym such as the Calf Pump or Arm Activation, to help her to focus and to feel her muscles and movement, and thereby to sense the boundaries of her own physical body. This feeling of physicality helps to provide the safety and containment for which Christina is always searching. We also do some Energy Exercises (Brain Buttons, Balance Buttons, or Earth Buttons), which further help her to be more grounded, present, aware, and physically comfortable.

In deciding which Brain Gym activity is appropriate at which time during the day, we simply notice when Christina appears to feel unsafe—that is, when her energy seems to be scattered and ungrounded. This is an indication that she needs to do some Energy Exercises. When she is physically out of bounds, a need for focus is indicated, and we do some Lengthening Activities.

We hold the intention that Christina will eventually be able to access this safety and grounding for herself, and we hope that the repeated kinesthetic experience will teach her that her own physical and emotional sensations can be experienced with comfort and containment. With this repeated experience, Christina may be able to establish her own limits and function more independently, with less guidance from the adults in her world. Christina has also begun to mediate her actions with spoken language. She does this with delight — another sign that she is better able to contain her needs in the moment.

Containing Needs Over Time

One of the ways in which Christina has begun to show herself capable of internalizing her own limits is by demonstrating an ability to delay gratification. She used to intensely demand immediate satisfaction of her needs. If she didn't get this satisfaction, she often lost control, showing us that she didn't trust us to follow through, and didn't know how to meet her own sensorily motivated needs. In the beginning, Christina would crouch down in a corner of the room to hide. Nowadays, she is able to mediate her experience with language and function more socially.

One morning, the students were outside on the playground for recess when Christina looked up and saw a yellow ball on the roof of the building. It was she who had accidentally thrown it there on a previous day. She looked at me as she pointed at the ball and said, "Christina want." I responded by saying, "Oh, I see Christina's ball is up on the roof. Christina wants ball."

Christina jumped up and down in anticipatory excitement and again stated, "Christina want ball!" I told her she would have to wait for Joe, the custodian, to walk by, so that she could ask him to get it down for her.

About three minutes later, Joe walked out of the building; Christina ran over to him and, jumping up and down in front of him, said, "Christina want ball!"

When Joe looked inquisitively at me, I pointed to the ball. He then said, "Oh, I'll get it for you." As he turned and walked away, Christina started to follow him. He turned, held up his hand to gesture for her not to follow him, and said, "You wait here. I'll get it for you."

Christina stopped where she was, stood waiting for about two minutes, and then started for the door that Joe had just entered. I pointed to the rooftop and told Christina to look up, as Joe was on top of the building. I chuckled inwardly because, from the expression on her face, it appeared that she might be thinking, "Yeah, right! People don't walk on top of buildings. I'm going to find Joe. He said he'd get my ball."

But just then, Joe yelled from the rooftop, "Christina, I have your ball." She turned and looked at me in confusion, so I pointed to the rooftop. When she saw Joe, she jumped up and down. I said, "Use your words. Tell Joe what you want."

Joe asked her what she wanted, and she said, "Christina want ball!" Joe said, "Here it comes," and started counting. As he counted, Christina responded with, "One, two, three!" Joe threw her the ball, and Christina ran off, gleefully bouncing it. I encouraged her to say thank you, and she loudly repeated, "Thank you!"

The use of language provides a critical way for children to mediate their feelings, express their needs appropriately, and suspend the urge to take instant action, while anticipating future reward or effect.

I find such delight in watching children like Christina learn to appropriately express their wants and desires. As they do this, they construct their own internal limits, experience the ability to anticipate gratification, and find their place in a structured, social world. This sense that a child develops of his or her own safe space gradually translates into a respect for other people's space as well. Christina is finding her own structure, and is beginning to learn how to meld her personal space with the invisible social boundaries of her peers.

Discovering a Personal Space: Scott

Ten-year-old Scott was a continuously moving ball of energy and sound. At first, Scott was unaware of his surroundings, ignoring other people in the room except for one or two adults and one other student—a boy he wanted to play with. Scott had no idea how to interact with this boy appropriately. He would push him down, lie on top of him, and, in an effort to hug him, would often start to choke him before one of the adults intervened.

I began by asking myself such questions as: *How can Scott feel more safe? How can he feel more comfortable in his surroundings? How can I appropriately provide him with the physical touch and the stimulation that he looks for with his inappropriate behaviors?* Scott's attention was scattered all over the place; he seemed unable to settle down. I hoped that, with the right kind of sensory stimulation, he would be able to slow down and discover a stronger sense of his own body—his weight, shape, and motion—and the boundaries of his own physical presence. My intention, too, was to give Scott permission to vocalize in place of acting out. It was clear to me that he understood much more than he was able to express verbally.

Since it had been my experience that Brain Gym facilitates the development of language and articulation, I began using some of the specific activities with Scott that could improve his expressive vocabulary. Scott liked some of the movements and didn't care for others, so I honored his preferences. His favorite Brain Gym activities were the Thinking Cap (to stimulate the ears for auditory perception), the Owl (to release tense neck muscles and relax the tendon-guard reflex), the various Buttons (to increase the awareness of movement in gravity), and the Cross Crawl (to activate both the right and the left cerebral hemispheres). When I did these preferred activities with Scott prior to any game we played, he was able to focus, listen, and really play with me. Otherwise, he seemed unable to relax and calm himself enough to follow my lead.

One of Scott's favorite play activities was Car-Car, from the Edu-K Visioncircles course. Standing behind Scott, I covered his eyes and "drove" him around the room by allowing him to lean back against me. This activity offered Scott a chance to slow down, to feel his weight and the shape of his body against me, and to feel his feet on the ground. Without his vision to rely on, Scott needed to settle back in to the slower, more grounded rhythm of muscle and motion. As he opened his eyes, Scott could now match his visual input to what he felt in his muscles. This "visual-kinesthetic match" made a big difference in Scott's ability to stay relaxed and present with me, instead having his attention scattered by every distraction. I watched with delight as Scott began to accept and enjoy the sensory experiences he needed in order to grow—the sensory experiences that he had previously so often avoided by his constant speed and agitation. Now he seemed to be here with me, and more available to learning.

After his Brain Gym session, another game that Scott espe-cially enjoyed was hand clapping. While we were seated on the floor facing each other, Scott would imitate the number of times that I clapped, including the rhythm I established. This imitation of my clapping gave Scott a chance to practice con-centrating. He needed to listen carefully to my rhythm and to focus fully on the game we played as he watched me. The auditory stimulation, coupled with the visual input, created a game that was both fun and full of sensory and kinesthetic learning. I find these hand-clapping rhythms to provide good practice for the development of phrasing for speech

Scott and I played other games with sounds: I imitated sounds that Scott made, and we made up noise sounds such as "ding ding ding," "ugh ugh ugh," "oh oh oh," and "yo yo yo," then connected these sounds to activities. We played with large buttons from the front of a coat, and as Scott's finger swirled around the face of a button we sang, "Ding ding ding, ugh ugh ugh, oh oh oh, yo yo yo." Our bodies swayed back

As a result of Brain Gym, Scott has shown a considerable
increase in his self-awareness and his sense of presence.

and forth, side to side, or in a figure eight motion as Scott sat
on the floor between my outstretched legs, using me as a back
support. Even Scott's sounds slowed down, now more frequently matching the rhythm of his body movement.

I played these games with Scott consistently, and saw him
make great progress over time — especially in his self-awareness and sense of physical presence. I believe that the Brain
Gym activities facilitated Scott's ability to attend to all the
immediate learning possible. The auditory-linguistic games
seemed especially important in helping him settle in, contain
his energy, and discover more of his sense of personal space.

Throughout the year that Scott was my student, he often
vocalized repetitive patterns of seemingly senseless sounds.
He would say, for example, "Doo-e-doo-e-doo-d-o-o-o-t-s ..."
I would imitate these patterns as precisely as I could for a
couple of weeks, then begin to add more sounds. In this way,
I was able to invite Scott into an exploration of language as
well as some of the fun music and rhythms of the fifties:
"Dooey dooey doo dots doo dots, doo wop, shoo bop, doo wop."
I offered Scott songs from this era for his music-listening time
during the day. After about three weeks of this game in which

I accepted Scott's speech patterns and interacted with him by repeating and elaborating on them, he gradually discontinued the apparently random perseveration of sounds, and no longer blurted out meaningless, disconnected syllables. I then eagerly invited Scott to "use your words" when he wanted something. This became an incredible process of self-discovery. Scott began to express himself more clearly and appropriately, and by the end of the year, he had begun to use words functionally.

Respecting the Space of Others

Scott's two areas of greatest growth have been his heightened level of comfort within his own body and his increased awareness of himself and those around him. As his sense of self has increased, his respect for other people's boundaries has also increased. Scott no longer grabs objects out of other children's hands, pushes them, or hugs them without invitation. His tantrums have decreased from as many as ten per day to only one or two per month.

Because of the decrease in his inappropriate behaviors, Scott was eventually able to independently take the classroom attendance down the hall to Jan, the school secretary, and then return to class. In fact, after getting off the bus at the classroom door, he would arrive reciting his morning routine: "Hi! Hi! Hi! Jan 'tendance. Jan 'tendance. Flags! 'Tendance. Flags!" Once Scott returned to the classroom, three of us (two students and I) would go outside to raise the American and California flags. Scott eagerly watched the flags wave in the breeze as he stood and flapped his own hands.

Sometimes, upon returning to the classroom, he wanted to play peekaboo with Sigrid, the paraeducator in the room. He would drape a shirt from the back of my chair over his head and say, "I see you!" He then peeked out and said, "Me chu [miss you] ... Aw ... me chu," as he elicited another hug.

As Scott continues to discover his personal space, he is gradually learning to interact playfully and more appropriately, not only with the other students in his classroom but with everyone in his environment. Even his eye movements have slowed down, darting less frequently around the room, and now even resting sometimes to meet another person's gaze. Scott's parents are immensely pleased with his growth, and have expressed deep gratitude for both the safe place that was created for their son and the self-discoveries that Scott was able to achieve while in my class. After only a year in my class, Scott graduated to another classroom, one where the emphasis is on fine-motor skills. There he has continued to progress.

Chapter 8

Reaching Beyond the Familiar

*E*ach time a child ventures to reach out beyond what he or she has previously known or done, a small miracle happens. In my classroom, now and then I'm privileged to witness such a miracle taking place among the children.

Swinging, Walking, and Talking: Aron

Aron's story demonstrates the importance of holding consistent expectations for a child and maintaining a consistent use of language as the child dares to go beyond his familiar skills and behaviors.

Each morning when he arrived at school, Aron would seek out two small toys to hold—one for each hand—and then walk around aimlessly while moving his head from side to side, paying no attention to the rapid movement of his hands nor to the other children in the room. Often he would turn the toys over and over again on a flat surface such as the floor or a desktop. The movement of the toys and the noise that they made flipping back and forth seemed to give him the constant stimulation he craved.

When I first met Aron, he would always be looking off into the distance, and would vocalize random sounds as he manipulated his toys. Following some in-depth Edu-K work with Dr. Paul Dennison that focused on Aron connecting his vision with his body movements, Aron began to actually look at what he was doing with his hands.

As the months passed, I watched with curiosity as Aron became increasingly more present with his own body movements. After about five months, he added a creative new dimension to his play. Though he continues to choose two toys with which to give himself stimulation, he now often picks up a blue, transparent sheet of paper and uses it as a place to focus as he flip-flops the toys back and forth on it. I imagine that the blue sheet provides a context, as well as visual contrast for what he's doing with his hands. Since Aron is now increasingly more aware of himself, and is connecting his vision with his own body movements, he has become more present with all of us in the classroom, and seems less often lost in some faraway world.

Since I've known Aron, I have made a continuous effort to help him increase his word approximations. When he drops a toy he has been playing with, I pick it up and ask him if he would like to continue to play with this toy. If his facial expression indicates yes, I prompt him by saying, "Toy, Aron. Say toy."

A fifth-grade peer tutor demonstrates to Aron
how to play a focusing game.

Aron reaches for the toy and again indicates yes with a longing look; again he is prompted. This often goes on four or five times, until Aron realizes that what I am asking him to do is say, "Toy." As soon as he attempts a sound that approximates the word "toy," I say, "Good, Aron. You said 'toy.' I am happy when you say what you want. Toy." And I give him the toy.

This interaction clearly indicates Aron's newfound ability to focus on an object, have a thought about wanting that object, and now even create a sound to request that object. It is my good fortune to be closely observing Aron's gradual language development—similar to an infant's process of language acquisition, and just as exciting. Through our interactions, Aron is learning how to think, and he has begun to use more and more word approximations. He is increasing his vocabulary of thoughts and his means of communicating these thoughts to others.

The Brain Gym activities we do with Aron in the classroom increase his ability to focus, to access speech, and to articulate words. Nowadays, we do the Receptive Owl, the Footflex, and the Calf Pump, intermittently throughout the day. Each time I do these movements with Aron, I also do them for myself. In this way, I experience benefits similar to Aron's while serving as a model for him.

Aron's word approximations have increased from zero to about three every hour. His mother notices that he is talking more, and is so impressed by the positive effect Brain Gym is having on Aron that she has taken a Brain Gym course herself, and is now doing Dennison Laterality Repatterning (DLR) with him at least once each week. I feel certain that this, too, has increased Aron's ability to understand and retrieve the words that he hears all day. Our hope for Aron, as he continues to reach beyond his familiar incessant mumbling, is that his vocabulary of thoughts and word approximations will continue to grow, and that more people will be able to understand him when he makes a statement or requests something that he desires or needs.

Not only has Aron increased his attempts to use understandable words, he also has worked diligently to improve his walking gait. Aron has very low muscle tone. He often reminds me of the lovable, ungainly scarecrow in *The Wizard of Oz*. Initially, his gait was uneven and he would sometimes unexpectedly throw an arm or leg up into the air and then continue on his way. For the first year and a half

Aron (seen here on the playground with Cece) has now learned to swing!

that I knew him, Aron was able to walk, but not run. He now runs along with me when I encourage him, his gait is more fluid and even, and the uncontrolled movements now occur more in the trunk of his body and less in his limbs.

During Aron's first year in my classroom, he was unable to sit on a swing. He was guided through daily DLR, and needed to be motored through the steps involved in riding on a swing. This was necessary because he had no understanding of how to use the quadricep muscles in his thighs to lift his feet off the ground. Now in his second year in my class, Aron swings willingly and joyfully when he is invited to do so. When given verbal cues such as the voice of an adult enthusiastically saying, "Swinging is fun!" Aron is able to stay upright on the swing and keep his feet off the ground for a full three minutes.

This newfound ability is quite remarkable, given what one might expect of an eight-year-old boy with such low muscle tone. In fact, Aron's mother, Lauren, was told that her son would never be able to walk. When he was two and one-half years old, she took him to Bob Doman, a consulting developmentalist in Los Angeles, California, who taught her how to do patterning with him. Lauren has told me that the year was very intense, with rigorous daily cross-crawling, and that it worked: Aron began to walk! The patterning training shows up whenever we do DLR with Aron; he seems to remember the cross-crawling he did six years ago, and he continues to enjoy the cross-lateral activities. It does my heart good to see him laugh and smile during the DLR.

Aron's recent ability to generalize this cross-crawling skill into a variety of different activities is inspiring. Both his walking and his running now appear to involve more use of postural muscles and more movement of opposite hips and shoulders—a dramatic shift from his former stilted and one-sided movement. One day, Sigrid was helping Aron up the stairs in the therapy unit, where we were spending some play-time. Previously, Aron would look down as he climbed the stairs, and would always lead with the same foot, in a one-sided fashion. There was no alternation of feet or matching of arm movements. This time, though, as Sigrid lifted his left hand and arm, Aron followed by placing his right foot on the next tread. Subsequently, as Sigrid moved Aron's right hand and arm onto the banister, Aron was able to independently lift his left foot and place it on the next tread. The two continued rhythmically climbing the stairs in this graceful cross-lateral motion.

I was filled with both delight and wonderment that Aron had generalized the cross-patterning to the skill of climbing stairs. My sense is that, as we continue with DLR and the Brain Gym activity known as the Cross Crawl on a regular basis, Aron will be able to more consistently monitor his gross-muscle movement while he is walking or running. As his whole-body movement becomes more coordinated, I trust that Aron's ability to differentiate for fine-motor skills will also improve.

Exploring the Small Joys of Life: Roni

Roni sings as she swings, sings as she goes down the slide, sings as she plays in the sand, and sings as she walks in the rain. When she was seven, the only outdoor play Roni enjoyed at school was riding on a swing. Fear kept her from exploring other playground toys and structures. Gradually, over our first four months together, she progressed to other activities, and as she did, I observed how important her singing voice is to her. I have come to understand that Roni feels more comfortable doing activities and exploring new things when there is a song attached. Without the singing, Roni's movement gets stuck in stops and starts. The rhythm of the sound seems to provide her with a context of meter and continuity that she needs in order to keep moving.

One day I sat on one of the little tricycles and began propelling myself (with my feet on the ground) around the play yard sidewalk as I sang this little ditty: "Riding is fun. I like to ride. Riding is fun. Will you ride with me? Riding is fun!"

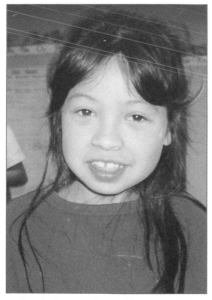

Roni sings to herself to provide her own rhythm for movement.

Roni called to me from across the play yard as she got off her swing, asking, "Can I play with you?"

"Sure," I said, "I'll help you find a bike." Roni sat down on the tricycle we found for her and followed me around the sidewalk, propelling herself the same way I was doing —feet on the ground—and singing the same little ditty. The principal came by just then, smiling as he shook his head at us in mock dismay.

A few days later, the physical therapist brought out a bigger tricycle that had an adhesive surface on the pedals, enabling Roni's feet to stay in place. Now Roni needed to learn how to use her quadricep muscles to propel the tricycle while moving the pedals. She expressed fear and said that it was too big. Yet, with laughter, song, and lots of encouragement from the therapist and me, she began pedaling the bigger tricycle on her own. Since she didn't know how to steer, I stayed right beside her and sang, "Roni's riding on the bike. Roni's riding on the bike."

Suddenly Roni realized what she was doing. She abruptly stopped her singing and cried out in fear: "Off! I want to get off!" I told her she was safe, and began singing again. I also pointed out a good place for her to get off on the other side of the play yard, another thirty feet away. Roni made it to the other side, pushing the pedals with great enthusiasm, and everyone praised her with smiles and laughter. Roni said, "I did a good job! I rode the bike!" Then she gleefully jumped off the tricycle to return to the swing.

Since that wondrous day, we have begun to do Hook-ups (to calm Roni) and the Cross Crawl (to activate her leg muscles and alternating gait reflexes) before Roni climbs onto the bigger tricycle. I do these same Brain Gym movements right along with her, and as I model the activities I also receive their beneficial effects. We still sing, yet the added Brain Gym movements seem to offer Roni a gentle impetus to reach beyond her familiar activities. She now often chooses to ride a tricycle rather than always going over to the swing. It's such great fun to see Roni exploring life like this!

Vision Training: Gaby

When I first met Gaby, I saw a shy, quiet seven-year-old girl with dark hair and large brown eyes. Because of a brain injury that affected her right side, Gaby's right eye is atrophied: the iris on that side is distorted, and smaller in size than that of her left eye. She reacts to hearing a voice by looking toward the speaker, and will almost always respond to my requests to engage in the activity at hand. Yet I observe that, if I did not enlist Gaby's attention, she would be very content to stay quietly in her own little world.

Gaby uses a wheelchair, yet can stand in a prone stander (a device that straps her in place so that she can't fall and can experience putting weight on her feet) for thirty-five minutes at a time. She has frequent seizures, and is dependent upon others for her personal-care needs.

In the classroom, I do Edu-K vision training with Gaby daily, using a ball that lights up and remembering to keep the sessions brief. I have found these methods to be universally applicable to the special-needs population. The following are some key points that I keep in mind before, during, and after Gaby's vision training.

1. I always check, through careful noticing of Gaby's breathing, sense of presence, and ability to focus, to see whether she is ready, willing, and able to accept new learning related to her patterns of visual movement.

2. I train for each visual skill (e.g., flexibility of near-to-far focus) for not more than one minute, so that Gaby is given time for integration. I support any changes she might be experiencing with positive feedback: "Good work, Gaby. I like the way you're following the light."

3. I am attentive to signs that Gaby might be tired, dizzy, or feeling disoriented during or after the training, simply by watching her responses and her length of concentration.

4. I remember that more is not better and that it's important to avoid eyestrain.

5. Daily, Sigrid and I engage Gaby in three-dimensional and distant visual activities, taking her outside for fresh air and

sunshine, and providing adequate light for her when we are involved in tabletop activities. All this encourages Gaby to use her vision more, rather than staring off into the distance or simply falling asleep.

6. Although Gaby wears her glasses and her hearing aid during the training, it appears that the intensive sensory information she receives when she wears them for hours at a time is simply too much for her. So, throughout the day, I intermittently remove them both to give her brief rest periods.

7. I consult regularly with the school's vision specialist so she can offer suggestions, validate improvements, and/or coach me in how I can further support Gaby's progress. I feel it's very important to allow information to come from different sources, although it is the Brain Gym activities that seem to create the longest-lasting and least-frustrating learning for Gaby.

I occasionally do a brief vision-training session with all ten children in the classroom. The process is shortened and simplified to accommodate both Gaby's particular needs and the more general needs of the other children in the class:

■ I check each day to see what color Gaby is least able to focus on, and use that color for the training. Some days this is the color red, some days blue. When Gaby is least able to focus on red, then I know she is probably having difficulty with tasks that involve near-visual skills. If blue is the color that it is harder for Gaby to focus on, then I know she is probably having difficulty seeing at a distance.

■ I also check the Edu-K points related to specific visual skills. These points facilitate the development of such skills as eye-teaming (binocularity); the ability to point the eyes together (convergence); the ability to track from one visual field to another across the visual midline (tracking); diagonal tracking for uneven (astigmatic) uses of the eye; and near-to-far and far-to-near swinging, to increase near-to-distant visual flexibility. I check Gaby to see which of these points she most needs to have stimulated during the session.

■ To begin the vision training, I turn off all the fluorescent lights in the classroom and turn on the halogen lamp at a dim setting, to create a feeling of calm. I put on some music (currently it's "Look Them in the Eye and Say Hi!" from Red Grammar's *Teaching Peace* cassette). After the children and I have listened to two rounds of this song, I turn off the halogen lamp and turn on the lighted makeup mirror. For the students who need less specific visual learning, I do all of the above actions with the mirror as I sing to each student (with Red Grammar's help), "I Think You're Wonderful!" During this time I also have one or two students working with the black light and all of the fluorescent cloth materials that show up so well under it. However, with Gaby, I use the lighted ball or a flashlight covered with the chosen color, and do all the Edu-K vision training with that color as I sing to her. It's amazing how each student will wait his or her turn for these visual games, and I find it heartwarming to hear the two students who have some language singing along with Red Grammar and me.

When we have completed these activities, I tell Gaby what a wonderful job she has done and let her know that we've finished the day's vision training. She then usually sits quietly, awaiting the next activity, and seems to settle comfortably in her wheelchair to participate in the remainder of group time while we pledge allegiance to the flag, take attendance, and do a language-arts lesson.

Gaby is getting stronger, as is evidenced by her improved health. During the time we have been doing the vision activities, her visual response has become smoother, her eyes appear better able to focus and work together, and her visual flexibility in different fields has increased. Gaby enjoys it when the

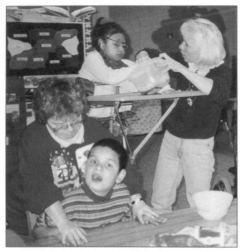

Gaby develops her fine-motor skills by making cookies with Cece.

general-ed peers come to assist her in her classroom projects, and expresses her joy by looking at them and smiling. Her mother has many times thanked me for the happiness on Gaby's face when she comes home from school. I feel so deeply satisfied when a parent gives me confirmation of progress I see in the classroom. I know that Gaby's school experiences are making a difference in this little girl's abilities, and it is a gift to me when her mother tells me that the effects are also rippling into Gaby's family life.

From Blindness to Sight: Jacob

When I first met Jacob, I could only wonder, *Oh my goodness, what do I do with this child? He can't see and he can't hear. How can I know what he wants, needs, or even likes?* As it turned out, Jacob's presence didn't justify my trepidation, for he was generally quite relaxed. Overall, he seemed content.

When I asked Jacob's mother about her hopes for her son, she gave a heartfelt sigh and said, "I only want him to be comfortable and happy." This modest expression of her hopes freed me of some of the strain of personal expectations I might have placed on myself with regard to Jacob's growth. Now I could look calmly at this little boy and begin to assess what he was actually capable of doing.

In my initial assessment, I thought, *Well, okay, if he can't see, he can't hear, he can't eat, and he can't tell me what he likes, then how will I find out what he* can *do?* When I heard myself asking this question, I realized that I had just taken the negative stance that so many teachers and practitioners in Jacob's life must have taken up to this point. I made up my mind to dig deeply into my own creativity for answers. I thought, *Well, I see what he can't do, and yet I don't know what he* can *do. So I'll start with all the Brain Gym Buttons, and see if this will allow him to feel more comfortable in his body.*

I began by holding the Earth Buttons, Space Buttons, Brain Buttons, and Balance Buttons for Jacob. Even these simple activities were too intrusively tactile for him: he would fuss, cry, and attempt to curl himself into a ball. I consulted Paul Dennison, who again encouraged me to "back up" into less tactile activities. This meant that I must consider the developmental stages of infancy or early childhood, so as to determine at which of these stages a child such as Jacob might still be functioning.

In "backing up," I gave Jacob many brief, gentle sensory experiences with scents, touch, lights, massage of his hands, musical instruments such as bells, maracas, and a tambourine, and eventually vibrational toys. As long as I went slowly and

softly, Jacob accepted these sensory experiences. His facial expression would be pensive, yet would show no evidence of fear. Soon, Jacob began accepting modified Cross Crawl movements in addition to the above sensory-stimulation activities. This stimulation of the senses had apparently been lacking in Jacob's world. His mother told me that he was now beginning to laugh and to keep his

Cece guides Jacob in a Double Doodle activity to enhance his binocular vision.

eyes open for longer periods of time. With the Cross Crawl movement and the sensory activities, Jacob now showed himself able to accept touch. So, after about three months of these types of stimulation, I introduced DLR.

Jacob received the repatterning with some resistance. On days when it was too stimulating for him, we would do the Cross Crawl only. I soon saw that the DLR had a significant effect on Jacob's ability to bear weight on his feet. Prior to the DLR, Cindy, the school physical therapist,

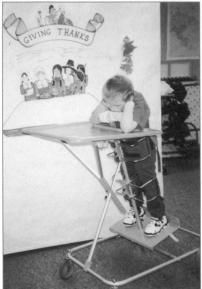

Standing in the prone stander is a new learning for Jacob, who first bore weight on his feet at age ten.

had guided me in techniques to facilitate Jacob's ability to bear weight, and Jacob had been kneeling prone over a ball daily for three months. After only three repatterning sessions, I saw such response in Jacob's attentiveness and muscle tone that I excitedly asked Cindy if Jacob could now attempt to stand prone over the ball. Her answer was yes.

First, I facilitated Jacob through DLR. I followed this with some Lengthening Activities, to release tense muscles and tendons. Then the therapist showed me how to place Jacob properly in an upright position against the ball, with his weight divided evenly between both of his feet. After two months of this daily activity, Jacob was able to bear weight on his feet for up to sixteen minutes while standing prone over the ball! These slow-but-steady gains require a sometimes tedious persistence, but my patience is more than rewarded when I see Jacob surpassing his former limits.

Jacob continues to make progress, receiving daily PACE and

Lengthening Activities and weekly DLR. His body is getting stronger. He can now stand in the Prone Stander for as long as thirty-five minutes at a time, and is able even to bear weight on his forearms when assisted with verbal and kinesthetic cues. He shows his delight in coming to school by smiling and laughing, and he loves to go outdoors and swing while seated on the wheelchair swing (a swing that allows a child to remain seated in a wheelchair while being pushed in it).

This learning is quite amazing when we consider that all Jacob did when he first arrived in my classroom was curl himself up in a ball, suckle on his lightly clenched fist, and cry when he was hungry or uncomfortable. Because he did not welcome any tactile stimulation, Jacob slept through much of his first year in my classroom. Furthermore, ophthalmologists had for nearly ten years declared him to be completely blind. However, when Jacob's mother came to an Open House early in Jacob's second year in my classroom, she brought me a dozen long-stemmed red roses to express her gratitude. She had just taken Jacob to an ophthalmologist, who determined that Jacob was no longer blind but nearsighted!

Jacob is still considered legally blind because of his depth astigmatism, however his vision is correctable to 40/40 when he wears his new eyeglasses. He now listens attentively when someone speaks to him, and his eyes roll back in his head much less frequently. I'm proud to say that these changes came about because I took the time to explore Jacob's unknown capabilities with him by way of gentle, specific Brain Gym and Edu-K vision-training activities.

I did the vision training daily with Jacob from the time he first arrived in my classroom, without any expectation that he would one day see; I simply followed my instincts and explored. Now my intention for Jacob, as for Gaby and all the other students, is to see if he can increase his ability to point his eyes together as a way to exercise the visual system and corresponding areas of the brain. After turning off all the fluorescent lights and turning on the black light, I place a fluorescent-colored cloth toy about ten inches from Jacob's face. In silence, I move the toy from left to right, vertically, in a Lazy 8 pattern, and in diagonal patterns.

In the early days, Jacob would respond very little. At first, he almost always had his eyes closed. Weeks of this daily stimulation went by, until he began opening his eyes for brief seconds. Those seconds were like a precious gift to me, and I challenged myself to patiently continue the activity. Supported by the encouraging and informative words of Cynthia, the school vision specialist, I began to understand more about what to look for in the training sessions. Ultimately, the many weeks of persistence caused Jacob to "wake up" parts of his brain that he had never used, and to begin to see the world!

Jacob's mother, Bettina, has said that in his entire life he "has never before had so much care and concern bestowed upon him." Judy, a veteran teacher in the school, saw Jacob in the swimming pool one day and was astounded. She remarked on how Jacob has become "a different little boy." Judy commented on how he had his arm draped over the swimming instructor's shoulder rather than curled in, and she noticed that he was alert and smiling as he hung on to the instructor.

A volunteering peer tutor motors Jacob (who until recently was considered blind) through an art project that emphasizes hand-eye coordination.

Jacob now is more curious and maintains visual contact for longer periods. His auditory perception has changed, as has his spatial perception as I move him from prone to sitting to other various positions. He definitely has a more grounded sense about himself, as is evidenced by the way he curls and uncurls his toes, by the lesser degree of flexion in the trunk of his body, and by his greater awareness of movement in his legs.

I find it a continual joy to witness these small miracles that happen as a result of the simple Brain Gym activities and a loving, caring environment—one where learning can take place for a child regardless of his or her level of functioning.

Recently, Jacob's younger brother, Jeremy, asked me if I could "wake up the part of Jacob's brain that could make him talk, and then wake up the part of his brain that could make him walk, and then wake up the part that could make him eat." Jeremy concluded, "Then he'd be a regular guy like me, and we could play together!"

With tears brimming in my eyes, I replied, "I'll do my best!"

Chapter 9

Bringing Out the Child's Gifts

arents often tell me that they sense what their child needs, yet can't always find the time or resources to follow their intuition and see that those needs are met. That is also true for me, as a teacher. When I have an opportunity to just stand back and observe a child, I often sense the possibilities and potential in his or her behavior, just as a parent might do. Yet I understand how it can be so much easier to simply repeat habits and behaviors that maintain the day-to-day routine.

There is no question that these children have many gifts to bestow. Yet sometimes the gifts come packaged in subtle or unusual wrappings, and some days I am just too tired to receive, or even to notice that learning is coming my way. At such times, I remember: that's okay. I remember to accept the fact that to feel tired, overwhelmed, or frustrated is to be human. Then I gather sustenance from friends, from my husband, or from other teachers, so that I can again be open to receive the wondrous blessings these children offer me, and the circle of giving can continue. These are the times when, rather than getting bogged down with expectations of what I can and can't do for a student, I remember the importance of valuing and supporting each child's unique personality and all his or her lessons and challenges in life.

In my classroom, I do my best to give the children space to explore. I establish boundaries of safety, and extend to

144

each child an invitation to grow and learn. I seek, at all times, to honor the gifts they bring to me. The only way I can do this is to bring the highest ideals I can to the joys, demands, and frustrations of the moment-to-moment classroom routine. You see, these children are my teachers just as much as I am theirs.

The children give me gifts that are simply amazing. They give me opportunities to discover the depth of my life, along with the depth of my character, commitment, abilities, and patience. They also give me the means to explore my spirit more deeply than I imagined possible. They invite me to go further than I would ever go on my own, inspiring me to work harder and to seek answers to many of the questions life poses. Sometimes they create questions for which I can find no answers.

These children bring me the gift of awareness—helping me to notice my own healthy back and legs and my ability to move my body freely, as I stand upright and independently put one foot in front of the other. These children offer me the treasure of simplicity, of letting go of the struggles and conflicts of my more complicated life and enjoying things as a child. I am learning from them how to "be" unconditional love, as they give me their innocent trust and depend on me for their every need. They teach me to respect the uniqueness of others and to appreciate the sanctity of life. They teach me about how very precious this life is and about valuing the small things. For the time I am with them, I can get out of my own way and simply "be"—be present, be available, be open to their love—and forget for those moments my own needs and desires and dreams. Their way of giving is such a gift; they model for me the very essence of giving.

Just as I am sharing stories with you about each of the children and some of the ways I encourage them to grow and learn, I also invite you to imagine the changing dynamics within the classroom. There are so many gifts offered there, and so many lessons learned.

More Music for Christina

As I grow and learn, so too do the children change. One time, for example, we were all in our daily circle time. Typically, we play and sing two songs at this time, with the help of the tape recorder. Well, on this particular morning, Christina wanted more singing. "More music," she commanded, using the few words available to her.

My immediate response was that the music was finished. It was time to go on to the next activity of reviewing the calendar. We would come back to the music, but now it was, I repeated, "time to do the calendar." Christina, who is still learning to use words to express her wishes, sometimes becomes nonverbal when angry or upset. She wanted more music, and ran over to the tape recorder to turn it on again. However, I pulled the tape out of the recorder before she could reach it. In frustration, she picked up the recorder and threw it to the ground— smashing it—and then huddled in the corner with her hands covering her face.

I went over to her, and because she had just broken our expensive classroom tape recorder, I was in an angry huff. Pointing to my chin, I said, "Look at this face. This is not a happy face. You will not break things in this classroom. That is my tape recorder! You do not throw my things!"

Christina reacted in kind. She lashed back at me, defending herself against my anger with her most basic skill: she bit me. My arm was throbbing and my feelings were hurt, yet through it all I saw a teachable moment for both myself and Christina. I asked one of the sixth-grade peer tutors, Monica, for help.

Christina was in a volatile place, so I cautioned Monica to keep a safe distance from her. I wanted her to maintain verbal contact with Christina while watching her body language for any signs of further aggression. In this way we communicated to Christina that, while her behavior was unacceptable, she was still an important person who deserved acceptance. As

Christina was able to focus over a five-week period to make a papier-mâché bowl for her family's Thanksgiving Day table.

Monica, at my suggestion, began to describe to Christina some things that make her feel angry and some acceptable ways that she expresses her anger, I iced my arm. I then returned to the circle to continue the day's lesson.

After about six minutes, Monica said that it seemed as if Christina was ready to join the circle again. As she came back to the circle, Christina said, "Sorry." My heart melted, and my eyes filled. I realized that I had set up a power struggle. Christina was only making a passionate request (even if inappropriately) when she ran to the tape recorder to play more music. I realized that I had forgotten to follow the children's needs, forgotten to consider classroom routine as secondary in importance to those needs.

Now, I remind myself to listen more to my students' emotional requests. As a result, some days we play twenty or more minutes of music during circle time, and never review the calendar. Those are the days that Christina or Roni say, "More," or "More music, please." Christina has brought me the gift of listening, and in return I give her space to express her desires.

147

The Joys of Learning: Youana

Because Youana was in school on a half-time basis due to health challenges, the Brain Gym activities that I first used with her were relatively limited. Because of her ceaseless motion, I initially decided to help her discover her body midline. I began with all of the Buttons, but Youana's ceaseless head swaying and the difficulty she had in breathing made it hard to hold a focus. I became discouraged by her lack of progress, and discontinued the Brain Gym movements.

But when Youana returned to school after a six-week absence necessitated by illness, she seemed stronger, more alert, and more inquisitive. I started putting her in the prone stander daily, but her neck muscles were so weak that she was unable to hold up her head. I introduced the Owl and the Brain Buttons, also massaging the points just below her clavicle and directly under her ears. My intention was to give Youana information on how to use the muscles in her neck, as well as to strengthen those muscles.

After only seven weeks of this activity, though still unable to keep her head from moving, Youana was able to hold it up unassisted for ten to fifteen seconds. I was very encouraged by this progress, and decided to reintroduce the other Brain Gym activities, starting again with the Brain, Earth, Space, and Balance Buttons. As I saw her respond to these with increased alertness, I added the Footflex and the Calf Pump, with the intention of helping her to access more language abilities. The first time I introduced Arm Activation, with the idea of improving her neck-muscle strength, Youana's eyes widened in such surprise that I wondered, *What just woke up in there?*

After about six months in my classroom, Youana learned to say one word. Her mother's eyes filled with tears of joy when, for the first time in her thirteen years of life, Youana was able to look at her and say "Mama." Now that Youana is stronger and her health is much better, she is able to focus for longer periods of time and truly enjoys coming to school full-time. She continues to rotate her head from side to side, still unable to hold it motionless for longer than two to three seconds. Yet she is more comfortable in her body, and she expresses her joy so jubilantly that it is impossible not to feel her happiness.

I believe that these improvements come from a number of sources, such as the Brain Gym activities, the wonderful loving care Youana receives at home, the relatively new program of standing and positioning in a side lyer, and the learning environment in the classroom. Life is complex; different avenues and interventions need to be explored at different times. After all, eating carrots is not our only recourse when we want to improve our eyesight. We might also take supplements, brighten the light in the room, do Brain Gym activities, or wear glasses. Many different modalities can be explored to find what is needed at a given time.

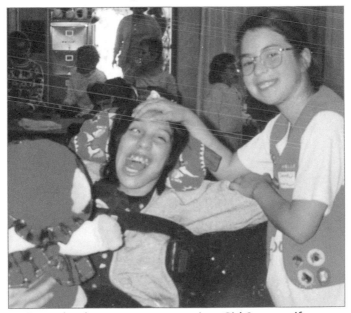

At a school party, a peer tutor in a Girl Scout uniform helps Youana stabilize her head movement so that Youana can take a closer look at a stuffed animal.

One thing is certain: Youana's eagerness and increased ability to learn, now that all of her energy isn't centered on her health, have contributed immensely to her quality of life! The following story illustrates the almost incredible speed with which she is learning new concepts this year.

Youana's mother works with her every night, assisting her daughter in doing her homework. I often send home reading and science homework for Youana to complete with her mother. Mom reads the book, which is a Spanish version, and Youana, in her own way, answers the questions at the end of each chapter. Now, anyone else might think, as they look at her work, that Youana is being assisted to write her name and then scribbling all over the page. Actually, Youana is being motored to draw pictures as best she can, in answer to each chapter's questions. She is so pleased and proud when I tell her, in English, what a wonderful job she has done.

It is clear that Youana has the benefit of a supportive atmosphere when doing her homework. Her mother's encouragement is simply unending, and Youana is blossoming. At school, since I am unable to speak Spanish but Youana has the ability to learn English, she is now learning math from me. In two weeks' time, she has learned the names of the numbers one through ten, as well as the one-to-one correspondence for numbers one through ten. For example, as I hold up three objects, Youana will say the number three. Sometimes I will hold up five fingers and ask, "Is this four?" Youana will make a facial expression to indicate "no." This is amazing progress. Youana learns math at home with her mom, in Spanish, then comes to school and learns more math in English.

Youana's math lesson at school is preceded by two Brain Gym activities—usually the Owl and the Calf Pump—which take about six minutes. The purpose of these activities is to enhance Youana's ability to hold spatial information in her memory.

In addition to the learning Youana is gathering in science, reading, and math, she is also continuing to learn to talk. The school's speech specialist, Nancy, has let me know that the encouragement I give Youana is working. She points out that Youana's sounds are nearly all vowels now, and that vowels are the first sounds a baby makes when beginning to speak.

Imagine how I feel when I hold up one finger and ask Youana, "How many fingers?" and she answers, "Uuunh." Then I hold up five fingers and she answers, "I-i-i-i." Then I say to Youana, "My name is Cece Freeman," and (pointing to another student) "Her name is Roni Burillo. What's your name?" And Youana says, "Uh-ah-ah Ma-ah-ah," and I say, "That's right! Youana Mahata! You are such a smart girl!" My eyes fill with tears of joy, and I wish I spoke Spanish so I could share Youana's triumph with her mother firsthand.

Blossoming Speech: Roni

Roni, now eight, spends more than a third of her day with general-education peers—in the classroom, outside at recess, and during lunch time. She plays appropriately, although she sometimes needs monitoring when she gets overly excited or gets stuck in repetitive phrases or actions. Other students sometimes feel frustrated with her when she imitates them or becomes obstinate in wanting her own way. Roni is exploring her world through this imitation, and learns by receiving immediate feedback, both from adults and from her general-ed friends.

Roni has learned to follow directions by looking for visual and gestural cues. For example, if I give her the directive, "Take this to Jan in the office, then come back to class," I have learned that Roni needs time to process the request. In the past, she would just stare at me unresponsively, and I would keep repeating the request. Now I wait silently for six or seven seconds, then pick up the envelope I want her to take to Jan, hold it up for her to see, and point to the door, then at Roni. Then I sometimes repeat the directive, but if I see Roni making motions to indicate she understands, I simply stand with a smile on my face, awaiting her approach. She repeats to herself as she takes the envelope from me, "Take this to Jan. Then come back to class." I say, "That's right, Roni. Good listening." Often she turns and spontaneously says, "I be right back!" as she joyfully heads out the door on her errand.

Now, let me back up a little in time. When Roni first entered my classroom, her expressive language consisted of only a few words, such as "Mommy," "Kimmy" (her sister), "school," "please," "thank you," "yes," "no," and "more." She was unwilling to participate in classroom activities; instead, she would sit in her chair or on the floor, acting frightened and frequently calling for her mother as tears filled her eyes.

For the first month that she was in class, each morning when she entered she would stand in one place, not even hanging up her jacket without verbal and physical prompting. She would then, with further prompting, choose a toy for independent play, and sit looking frightened as she watched the rest of the students arrive. Roni showed no interest in painting, using chalk, or doing pencil-and-paper tasks. Her favorite toy was a set of one-inch-high, brightly colored plastic teddy bears that

Roni has blossomed from a silent, frightened child into a smiling, more self-confident girl.

she would simply move around from place to place in front of her. Her walking gait was wide, legs spread apart to stabilize her movement. She thrust out her tongue in order to concentrate. As she moved her head, her neck muscles were tense and stiff. Even with orthotics (special arch supports) in her shoes, her feet tended to overpronate (roll toward the outside), and her foot placement was heavy.

She held her arms away from her body, often bent at the elbows. Roni would cry if another student took something from her. For example, if a classmate were to take a toy or book, Roni would repeatedly say "Mommy" and pout with tears in her eyes.

Toward the end of her first year in my class, Roni began to participate, to the best of her ability, in all classroom activities. These days, she will often say, when one activity is complete, "What are we gonna do now?" She will also ask questions about the other students in the room: if Jacob is crying, Roni will ask, "Whatsa matter with Jacob?" She still needs assistance in bathrooming herself and is not yet independent in getting dressed, but Roni is now able to come into the classroom, hang up her jacket, go to the cupboard, and independently choose a toy to play with while others arrive from the bus.

All in all, Roni's progress has been phenomenal. She goes to the general-ed campus when her peers from the third grade come to pick her up. Before she leaves the room, I ask her, "What is Roni going to do?" and she answers, "I do my best!" This learning came from an Edu-K balance I facilitated for Roni during her first year with me. The goal was "to relax and do my best." This balance came about because Roni was in trouble almost constantly for pinching, biting, and hair-pulling while out on the playground. I have observed that Roni resorts to these behaviors when she is overexcited; perhaps this is her way of releasing the mounting tension in her body. After the balance Roni seemed to to be more aware and present, and therefore more able to control her negative behaviors.

Roni continues to pinch occasionally (two or three times a month) when her peers forget to say with sufficient frequency, "I see Roni do her best; I am doing my best too," or when she gets overstimulated, but she no longer bites or pulls hair. This is a major shift, and the teacher on playground duty is quite delighted.

153

Roni is blessed by the friendship of a certain parent, Joan (the mother of one of the general-ed students), who regularly volunteers for playground duty. This kind woman will sometimes sit and converse with Roni during lunch, broadening her horizons and cueing her as to appropriate behavior at the lunch table. Joan also teaches Roni, helping her to review her counting and her ABCs and coaching her on how to respond when someone talks with her. Roni's progress from this quality time is very apparent. When she repeats language or actions that she has learned from Joan, she receives smiles and positive words from me or the class paraeducator Sigrid, and the new behaviors often then become a part of Roni's repertoire of words and actions. It's a joy to see this unfolding of Roni's learning.

I would now like to share with you the sensorimotor activities that I believe were central to Roni's shift in opening to her surroundings and to the people in her world.

My first intention, as Roni's teacher, was to create for her a feeling of personal safety in the classroom. During our first year together, we began by doing some Brain Gym activities once each day. For example, we often started with PACE to help Roni increase her awareness of her own centering and physical space. Next, we'd do the Thinking Cap and the Receptive Owl for memory, thinking skills, and clear listening. We also did Lazy 8s and Alphabet 8s (using the letters "a" and "b" and the letters of Roni's name) to increase her visual flexibility.

After seven months, we made a major addition to Roni's Brain Gym activities: daily Dennison Laterality Repatterning (DLR), with the goal of Roni being comfortable and feeling physically safe. We followed up with fun, creative exercises to reinforce the integration of expressive and receptive modalities, again emphasizing listening and speaking skills, as described below:

- motoring Roni through simple hand clapping, then clapping a rhythm, then having her mirror my clapping

- making noise sounds such as "ding ding ding," "ugh ugh ugh," "oh oh oh," and "yo yo yo"

- combining noise sounds with other activities, to coordinate listening and speaking with body movement

- feeling shirt buttons while making a different sound for each button

I also invited any insights and observations from Nancy, the speech specialist, with regard to Roni's language acquisition and how I might foster it. Nancy was very supportive of the activities I was already doing with Roni. When she worked with Roni one-on-one, her focus was to increase Roni's clarity of speech. Roni is very readily understood by me and the paraeducators in the room, yet her peers sometimes mock her lack of articulation or simply have difficulty understanding her requests or verbal exchanges. When Nancy and I recall her former teary-eyed fright and unwillingness even to join her peers on the playground, we are both thrilled with Roni's new willingness and ability to voice her preferences. In fact, only last year Roni would back herself up against the wall of the school building, with her body rigid and fear on her face, unable to voice anything, and now she leaves my classroom with the general-ed peers and walks enthusiastically to the other campus. If you didn't know Roni, you'd have difficulty distinguishing her from the rest of the crowd in the school yard.

The other major Edu-K activity that I used last year was the Goal Wheel. This is an elegant system for quickly, accurately, and nonintrusively identifying key issues or challenges related to any given situation. I came to the realization that I could assist Roni in opening to her world, not by thinking about what might be the source or the cause of her pinching and biting, but by using the Edu-K Goal Wheel. Through it,

I could ask Roni indirectly (since she was unable to voice her feelings), "What is the feeling that fosters this negative behavior?"

With skillful noticing, I could determine which issues of the Goal Wheel Roni was working on. I could then set up an appropriate intention to help her address her specific fear or challenge. This is an empowering method to use, as I find it allows me to set aside my own distracting thoughts and gently enter Roni's world. Once I determine the issue and set up the goal, I proceed with the Five-Step Balance process, with the only exception being that I modify the Brain Gym activities. Sometimes I even do the activities for Roni when they are too difficult for her, with the intention of becoming a sensory model for her. This way, when she needs, for example, to access more of her autonomic system through repatterning, I do repatterning for her, and then take the increased ability to simultaneously move and think into my interaction with Roni.

The Seven Dimensions Balance process allows me to determine what systems of the physiology — muscular, skeletal, chemical, emotional, respiratory, and so on — are most involved with Roni's immediate behavior. Remarkably, there is always an immediate shift in Roni's ability to relax and do her best, as is evidenced by the decrease in pinching, biting, and hair-pulling and by the joy with which Roni now leaves my classroom to go with her general-ed peers. I am still amazed by the ease, grace, and effectiveness of this balance process; the possibilities for its application seem endless.

Nowadays, as soon as the general-ed peers arrive for the half hour they spend in our class each day, Roni loudly announces, "Time to do PACE!" It puts a smile on my face. The third-grade classroom that Roni participates in every day also does Brain Gym regularly, so Roni also sees it used in the world outside of her special day class. Her mother says that Roni's growth inspires her. As for me, it warms my heart.

Connecting Vision With Body Movement: Ruthie

Ruthie's eyes would "bounce" excessively whenever she looked at something at close range, or even at the normal reading distance of about sixteen inches away. (This rapid, involuntary oscillation of the eyeballs is known as a nystagmus.) I began Ruthie's school year with Brain Gym activities that would focus on her ability to connect her vision with her hand movements. We also started the year with all the Buttons, to facilitate Ruthie's awareness of her own vertical movement in gravity and to help her become more relaxed. Therefore, her learning menu consisted of the Cross Crawl, the Brain Buttons, the Earth Buttons, the Space Buttons, the Balance Buttons, and Car-Car.

For Car-Car, the activity from the Edu-K Visioncircles course that I modified to accommodate Ruthie in her wheelchair, I cover her eyes with my hands from behind and "drive" her around the room as I tell her which way we're going: straight ahead, right, left, or backwards. The intention is, again,

Cece assists Ruthie in adding some new
sight words to her reading vocabulary.

to create an opportunity for Ruthie to learn to connect her vision with her muscle proprioception.

Over time, I have added the Thinking Cap, so that Ruthie can listen more attentively; Lazy 8s, to help her move her eyes more easily across the midline as she reads; Alphabet 8s, to help Ruthie experience the similarities of the letters and to activate various visual fields as she writes; and the Receptive Owl, to increase her neck relaxation and listening ability.

Ruthie's greatest changes have been demonstrated every time she has done Lazy 8s or Alphabet 8s. Often I have found her sitting at her desk, practicing her Lazy 8s and then her name. If she hasn't done the Lazy 8s first, she will write her name as follows:

After about 45 seconds of the Lazy 8s, she will write:

Initially, I was discouraged that Ruthie wasn't able to "hold" or retain the learning to the extent that she could correctly write her name without doing any preliminary Brain Gym activities. Yet Ruthie has taught me how to be persistent and patient. Through her sincere willingness—every single time—to practice Lazy 8s prior to writing her name, I have come to see what a blessing Brain Gym is. Ruthie has taught me that all I have to do is use it: through the example she sets, she reminds me to practice my own Brain Gym!

As the school year progressed, I began doing two more Brain Gym activities with Ruthie to further integrate her vision with her body movements: DLR and vision training (for convergence, tracking, far/near swing, etc.).

Ruthie has made noticeable progress in the level of comfort with which she looks at a page in order to read it. As of the end of this academic year, she has more than thirty sight words to her credit, and she now enjoys practicing her writing and spelling. Ruthie has far surpassed the goals set for her. Best of all, she is learning to feel good about herself and to assert her independence in a healthy way.

The Gifts My Students Share

Rudy gives me simplicity; Youana shares with me her joy. Scott gives me his charming way of showing affection; Roni gifts me with cute remarks, and reminds me how important it is to be consistent. Casey shares his heartfelt gaze; Aron lets me enjoy his delightful happiness. Jacob offers me pensive wisdom and a reminder that, sometimes, I need to invite people to participate in life; Lindsey gives me courage, and has shown me a reason to believe. Christina's gift is to remind me of the importance of firm boundaries, within which one finds freedom; Gaby's is the ease she feels in her body after we do movement.

It is an honor for us all, as a whole class of students, para-educators, and teacher, to be sharing this ongoing classroom life that is so very rich in life's lessons, life's gifts.

Chapter 10
Working Through My Own Issues in the Classroom

Most of the time, I feel as if I'm doing a great job. Yet sometimes, as I approach the school building in the early morning, I'm overcome by a feeling of dread and a flurry of negative emotions. At such moments, I don't even want to go into the building!

I love my job. I know that the children feel safe, comfortable, and loved. Their parents appreciate me. They express their gratitude with letters and phone calls; on one Open House night I even received a dozen long-stemmed roses from a thankful parent. What, then, is this feeling about? It's about the work environment.

I remember how, during my early years of teaching, I lost some of my enthusiasm for the job as I learned to find my way through the maze of bureaucratic rules that is an inevitable part of any school system. I was taken aback by the apathy of many of my colleagues who had been teaching for ten or twenty years. And back in 1980 the local administration seemed to focus more on district regulations than on the best interests of the students.

Sometimes there are still days when, as I approach the school building, the recurring theme of "education as a business vs. education for the child" causes me misgivings. Yes, I often experience the satisfaction that comes to all teachers who hold dreams and visions for the children in their classrooms. Yet, three thousand miles and nearly twenty years from my first teaching situation, I am still concerned that those dreams might be stifled by a blanket of administrative complacency.

My wish is not that others in the school system might think as I do or do as I do, but rather that each one of us who works in the field of education might be open to ideas and techniques that are new or different. In my own work, as I follow the school district's suggested curriculum I also seek out ways to meet the varied individual needs of my students. Still, the oppressive experience of exploring innovative methods in a climate of mistrust for the "new" has sometimes caused me to doubt myself, my work, and the sensory-based way that I've set up the program in my classroom.

Since my students are significantly delayed in their mental and emotional ages, part of the requisite curriculum in my classroom is the teaching of life skills—what the traditional educational model might call "academics." In many classrooms for children who have special needs, these life-skill lessons translate primarily into hand-over-hand motoring of students through the making of simple cut-and-paste projects. Children "turn out" art projects that the teacher and paraeducators meticulously set up ahead of time. I believe that the rationale behind this is that repetition reinforces behavior.

Although I, too, offer my students many of these table-top activities, my interpretation of life skills includes and empha-sizes the more basic sensory skills described in this book. This means that I need to be available to work spontaneously with my students in the moment—to follow their lead in whatever situation arises. Teachers and parents of preschool children generally create a child-centered atmosphere with much greater ease than do teachers of older children, who may rely on curriculum or agenda rather than heeding the children's needs for play and interaction. In the child-centered approach, the learning is body-based, emerging from the child's own exploration of the sensory world and its physical dimensions.

I know that I'm a person who needs to live what she believes. I see these children as expressing developmental needs that are of a preschool level. It makes sense to me to focus on the acquisition of the visual, auditory, tactile, emotional, social, and kinesthetic skills appropriate to the unfolding character of the child. I am realistic enough to know that the system won't change overnight—if at all. Therefore, I live with a disparity of ideas that causes me a certain amount of conflict and tension. I use the conflict to further my self-knowledge and to deepen my compassion and understanding. Then, by implementing Brain Gym for myself consistently throughout the day, I am able to slow down, focus, stay centered in my own experience, and let go of my thoughts in order to really listen to others.

Following the Students' Lead

Let me share an example of how I stay open and alert to the child's needs of the moment. It was the part of the day when we gather in a circle for our calendar time. When I walked to the front of the group, I saw that Christina had taken off her shoes and socks, which had resulted in a small pile of dirt on the floor in front of her. As I stood watching Christina, I took a moment to slow down and catch my breath, and briefly did the Brain Buttons movement for clarity of mind. I thought, *Hmmm, we certainly don't want* this *to become a habit. Now, why would Christina take off her shoes like that, when she never did before? Oh, I see: she had dirt in her shoes from recess. Makes sense to me; I'd empty my shoes if they were full of dirt.*

Meanwhile, Christina was still sitting in her chair, only now she was leaning over, picking up the dirt in her fingers, and starting to eat it. I saw the peer tutors and paraeducators looking to me expectantly for direction; the repugnance they felt at Christina's actions was evident on their faces. In my mind, I rapidly searched for the most effective way to address the situation:

How can I acknowledge Christina and also draw her away from this unacceptable behavior? How can I be fully present with this situation, respond to it, and still model flexibility and respect?

I realize that when I live with an attitude of curiosity, spontaneity, and respect for myself and each child or adult with whom I work, I can stay conscious about remaining in the process of life, and connected with the unfolding event. When I think I have to control, change, or stop what is happening, I am no longer open to my own feelings—no longer present for the process.

In the midst of this dilemma, I found myself able to stay open and alert to a "teachable moment." So I said, as I stood in front of the group, "Christina, do you know what they say about people who eat dirt?" She looked at me questioningly, and I said, "They say that they need more minerals in their diet."

Christina continued to look at me quizzically, but she stopped eating the dirt. *Okay,* I thought, *so I've got her attention.* I then said, "I see you've removed your shoes. I would take off my shoes, too, if they were full of dirt. Now, let's see if we can dump out the rest of the dirt so you can put your socks and shoes back on." For the next six minutes, I continued with a lesson centering around Christina's shoes and socks.

Picking up the socks, I shook them out, pretended to sniff them, and, in an exaggerated way, acted as if they were smelly. Everyone laughed, including Christina. I then asked, "What color are these pink socks?" One student said, "Pink!" "That's right!" I said. "How many socks am I holding up?" Another student answered, "Two!" Together, we then found Christina's right sock to put her right foot into, and of course the remaining sock was waiting to be put on her left foot, the foot that was left. I then picked up Christina's shoes and asked, "How many shoes are there in my hand?" Youana answered, "Two!" and we proceeded to match up the shoes for Christina's feet in the same manner in which we had found the right sock and the left sock.

When we were done, Christina had her shoes and socks back on and was comfortable, and we had all shared a lesson in counting, in color recognition, in one-to-one correspondence (one foot, one sock; two feet, two socks), in left/right body-part identification, and in noticing that everyone in the circle had two feet and that socks and shoes go on feet. Everyone was relaxed and happy, and we returned to the calendar lesson.

The more traditional approach might have been to take the attitude: "I'm the teacher and you're the student. Therefore, you'll do as I say. You must fit your needs into my lesson and my schedule." Other teachers at my school, observing my methods, have sometimes given me feedback to the effect that I allow the students to run the class, with the implication that I'm not in control. I disagree. In fact, I see my classroom as a small community, with no boss or hierarchy in the traditional sense. The aides and paraeducators are my co-workers. The students are my teachers, just as much as I am their teacher. I feel that we are all in the process of learning how to learn, learning how to be better human beings, and that there need be no power struggle—rather, a continuum of learning that takes place for everyone.

As the teacher, I am responsible for setting up the daily lessons, maintaining the flow of the classroom schedule, and doing my best to meet each child's needs. Therefore, my class-room is a very structured environment, with many different activities going on simultaneously. My students, with their unique personalities, surprising gifts, and active curiosities, are the focal point: the place where all learning begins and ends. You see, what I was really teaching (and learning) in that lesson with Christina's shoes and socks had much more to do with modeling problem-solving than with counting, identifying colors, and so on. I, as the teacher, was faced with a problem. Would I ignore it, react to it emotionally, or work with it?

I have found it to be essential to stay present with what's real, which I define as whatever is happening for myself and my students at any given time. My teaching style is human and heartfelt, and I know that it works. I have learned to accept that, as the teacher, I often need to let go of my own agenda and even my idea of order, to follow my students' lead. This is not always easy, as it often brings up my own emotional issues to be attended to. Yet I do my best. Since I continue to have the personal benefit of the Brain Gym movements and of Edu-K balances as these issues spontaneously arise, I sometimes gain a deep insight into the origins of my own agenda or the reason I might be imposing it.

Believing in Self

I'm a person who questions everything, and that includes questioning how my own actions affect others. The good news about all this questioning is that it can blossom into vigilance: to be of service, to stay in my integrity, and to have the courage to hold to my truth when I feel misunderstood. Yet this ongoing vigilance does cause me to feel weary at times.

My self-questioning about the methods and techniques that I use in the classroom continues in a cyclical way. I see the students looking happy, becoming more physically comfortable, learning about boundaries, and being willing to challenge themselves to grow and learn. And yet I ask myself, *Am I meeting their greatest needs, their deepest needs?*

I yearn for models to follow in the classroom; I consult with teachers countywide as well as in my school building. Yet always I must come back to the fact that this is my classroom, a place for me to set up an environment that I am comfortable with: one that will meet the needs of each one of these very individual children and also harmonize with my personality.

I remember what a hospice patient said to me one time: "Cece, maybe you could be a little less attached to the outcome and, in doing so, be more available for the process." Ahhh, yes

165

… And, with that reminder, I would like to share with you an encouraging classroom experience.

When this episode took place, Roni had been going to the general-ed campus for more than one-third of the day, including lunch and recess time, throughout the school year. As I've previously described, Roni often gets overexcited; when she does, she becomes impulsive and unable to maintain her personal boundaries. More specifically, she then has a hard time keeping her hands to herself.

One week, I had to restrict Roni from the general-ed campus because of this behavior. One day during that week, I used my break time to stay on the playground and facilitate a balance with her, one that specifically addressed the seven dimensions of intelligence.

Roni sat on the grass, randomly saying unkind things to the adults and general-ed peers around her, such as, "You stink" or "I don't want to do anything more because you're a baby." She was feeling quite rigid and very self-involved, as demonstrated by her unwillingness to look anywhere but at the ground in front of her. The goal for the balance was "to play like a sweet girl."

As we went through the balance, I followed Roni around the playground and invited her to do the Brain Gym activities called for by integrating them into her play. During those twenty minutes, I saw Roni begin to mellow into a feeling of comfort. She started to sing as she swung on the swing. She also began looking around and curiously asking in a friendly way about the other students on the playground. She even inquired about a girl who was out sick that day: "Where's Gaby? I don't see Gaby. Do you see Gaby?"

Throughout Roni's day at school, we now follow up the balance with intermittent Brain Gym activities. We also occasionally say to her, "Roni is a sweet girl. I like nice girls. Roni is a nice girl." The shift in Roni's self-awareness from this brief balance is so great that I gently remind myself: *I need to use this Edu-K tool more often.*

Once again I am being shown that, when I trust my intuition and use the tools that I've seen make a difference in the lives of these children, my resulting self-confidence flows into the class-room atmosphere and everyone is happier. It is in serving others that I find meaning in my own life, for when I seek to teach, to heal, to be of service to the children in my class, I myself am taught, healed, and served. As Paul Dennison eloquently states it: "The teacher must heal. The healer must teach."

Some Closing Words...

As my second year of teaching these children comes to a close, I reflect on the wonderful learning that has happened for each child—despite the fact that each had been labeled as severely handicapped. Rudy no longer arrives and departs in a wheelchair; Ruthie has learned to write her name correctly and has more than thirty sight words; Youana has begun to understand both English and Spanish and has started to attend school on a full-day schedule; Scott can slow down and express his needs without screaming or running out of the room; Roni has begun using speech and can actually sing "You're a Grand Old Flag" entirely by herself (the sounds are distorted, yet it's clear what song she's singing).

Casey looks lovingly at me when I sing to him; Aron has learned to pick up his feet so he can swing, and has begun to come when called; Jacob has learned to bear weight on his feet, and has begun to see; Lindsey's sight has partially returned, and she has gone back to her regular classroom with much less anger about her challenges; Christina has learned to focus her energies a little bit more; and Gaby is now able to be more alert and aware of her surroundings. Many of these children, who never before interacted socially as a group, now do so. When I consider these achievements that my students and I have accomplished together during these past two years, I am left with a glowing feeling of satisfaction and love.

I warmly invite all parents and teachers of children who have special needs to discover this cooperative way of working together, and to accept the many gifts that these children so freely offer us. These gifts include: opportunities to discover the depth of life, as we discover the depth of our patience, character, commitment, and abilities; the chance to explore our spirit more deeply than we imagined possible; an awareness of the great good fortune we have in our independence, in our healthy backs and legs, in our ability to do for ourselves—to stand upright and put one foot in front of the other. Perhaps most important of all, these children are able to give us faith in our shared human potential.

Also to be found among the innumerable gifts these children offer is an awareness of the value of simplicity. Through this gift, we can come to find joy in such simple things as knowing how much it means when we put our arms around them. The gifts include, as well, these treasures: a sense of mutual unconditional love; the children's innocent trust and dependency upon us; our own renewed respect for others and for their uniqueness; a heightened appreciation for the sanctity of life and for life's preciousness. The children hold something invaluable in store for us: they can teach us how to forget, for a while, our own needs and desires, so that we can experience the freedom and the rewards of true, selfless giving.

Key Brain Gym Movements That Enhance Specific Developmental Skills*

As Modified for Use With Children Who Have Special Needs

The Lengthening Activities

During the first five months of life, the survival mechanism housed in the brainstem develops so as to take in sensory data from the environment. When placed in new situations where there is too much information or where there is a perception of endangerment, the mechanism will trigger the organism to respond by drawing back until there is sufficient comfort to proceed. This contraction (called the tendon-guard reflex) affects posture by shortening the tendons in the back of the body from head to heels, thus confounding locomotion (self-initiated movement) and flexibility and blocking the flow of blood and lymph. The Brain Gym Lengthening Activities help to relax these muscles and tendons, increasing the learner's kinesthetic sense (the awareness of muscles and movement).

---

* This partial list of Brain Gym activities offers descriptions and applications adapted from *Brain Gym® Teacher's Edition* by Dennison and Dennison (1989). All of the information in this section has been taken from that book; for further understanding of the Brain Gym movements, please refer to the same. Although other Brain Gym and Vision Gym™ activities were used with Cece's students, included here are those activities that can be used and easily adapted by the layperson who is new to this methodology. Brain Gym® is a registered trademark of the Educational Kinesiology Foundation, (800) 356-2109.

Use of the Lengthening Activities helps to integrate neuro-developmental reflexes for the Focus (back-to-front) Dimension of movement, including the ability to roll from a prone to a supine position and vice versa; the ability to release tendons and relax one's muscles; and the ability to differentiate body areas and initiate movement from one part of the body. The Lengthening Activities help the individual learn to anticipate and plan ahead at the physical level; they have been found to help with speech, comprehension, and specific language disabilities, as well as with hypo- and hyperactivity.

The Receptive Owl

The Receptive Owl movement addresses visual, auditory, and head-turning skills. The process lengthens neck and shoulder muscles, restoring range of motion to the muscles and circulation of blood to the brain for improved focus, attention, and memory skills. It may also help relax habits of subvocalization. *To do the Receptive Owl, the teacher stands behind the student and squeezes the student's upper shoulders, while encouraging the student to turn his head to the left and right.*

This movement activates the brain for:

- integration of the tonic neck reflex

- release of the upper trapezius (shoulder) muscle, for better head and neck alignment

- crossing the "auditory midline" (auditory attention, discrimination, and perception)

- short- and long-term memory

- listening to the sound of one's own voice

- silent speech and thinking ability

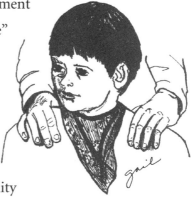

171

- more efficient saccadic eye movements
- integration of vision and listening with whole-body movement

Arm Activation

Arm Activation is an isometric activity that lengthens the muscles of the upper arms, upper chest, and shoulders. Muscular control for gross-motor activities (for throwing, catching, and so on) depends on proprioception of arm motion in a full range of positions, originating in the areas released by the Arm Activation. If these muscles are shortened from tension, activities related to fine-motor control (such as writing and the controlled use of tools) are inhibited. *The teacher lifts both of the student's arms straight up, holding them gently against the sides of his head, lengthening them, and lifting them slightly up from the rib cage.*

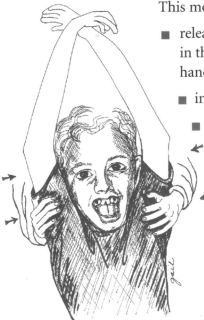

This movement activates the brain for:

- release of gross-motor tensions in the shoulders, chest, arms, and hands
- increased lymphatic stimulation
- enhanced postural awareness
- eye-hand coordination and the manipulation of tools
- expressive speech and language ability
- relaxed use of the diaphragm and improved respiration

The Footflex

The Footflex is a movement re-education process to restore the natural length of the tendons in the feet, ankles, and lower legs. These tendons shorten to protect the individual from perceived danger, a response caused by the tendon-guard reflex, which is a brain reflex to withdraw or to hold back. *The teacher holds the origin and insertion of the muscles of the front and back of the calf, one at a time, in the lengthened position. She simultaneously moves the foot into its pointed and flexed positions. Repeat with the other calf and foot.*

This movement activates the brain for:

- back-front integration of movement (the ability to hold back as well as to self-start)

- improved weight bearing

- enhanced postural awareness

- increased lymphatic stimulation

- relaxation of hyperactivity and hypervigilance

- enhanced self-expression

- expressive speech and language skills

The Calf Pump

The Calf Pump, like the Footflex, is a movement re-education process to restore the natural length of the tendons in the feet, ankles, and lower legs. This activity is done with students who can bear weight on both feet. The student stands at arm's length from a table and leans toward it, resting on her palms. One leg is extended straight out behind her, so that the ball of her foot is on the floor and her heel is off the floor. *The teacher holds the student's ankle while gently pressing the child's heel down toward the floor. She then raises the student's heel, and repeats this pressing and raising process several times, thereby lengthening the calf muscle. Repeat the movement with the other foot.*

This movement activates the brain for:

- back-front integration of movement (the ability to hold back as well as to self-start)
- improved weight bearing
- enhanced postural awareness
- increased lymphatic stimulation
- relaxation of hyperactivity and hypervigilance
- enhanced self-expression
- expressive speech and language ability

The Energy Exercises

The Energy Exercises validate important tactile and kines-thetic information about inner-body relationships, especially for all up-and-down movements such as sitting, standing, rising up on the toes, and even the more subtle movements of breath-ing, swallowing, and eliminating. This sense of verticality in gravity establishes a basis for directionality and an awareness of where we are in space, as well as of the location of objects in our environment and our relationship to them. When visual skills are built on this proprioceptive foundation, a match is easily made between what is seen and what is experienced. Without this congruency, conflict among the sensory channels makes learning difficult.

Use of the Energy Exercises and the postures for Deepening Attitudes helps to integrate: neurodevelopmental reflexes for centering, basic to vestibular balance and equilibrium; sensi-tivity for touch or sound; the mechanics of speech, sucking, swallowing, and articulation; mature digestion and assimilation; visual-perceptual organization; and the sense of pace, which is the student's own rhythm and timing.

Water

Water is an essential conductor of electrical energy. Two-thirds of the human body (about 70 percent) is made up of water. All of the electrical and chemical actions of the brain and central nervous system are dependent on the conductivity of electrical currents between the brain and the sensory organs. This conductivity is facilitated by the presence of water in the body, yet stress dehydrates the body. Like rain falling on the ground, water is best absorbed by the body in frequent small amounts. *The teacher and student sip water as they work together, and when possible also include in their diets foods that have a high water content.*

Drinking water activates the brain for:

- efficient electrical and chemical action between the brain and the nervous system
- cleansing of the lymphatic system (especially important during times of excessive sitting)
- more efficient storage and retrieval of information

The Brain Buttons

The Brain Buttons increase the supply of blood and oxygen to the brain and help to release visual stress related to crossing the midline. *With one hand, the teacher firmly massages the soft tissue under the student's clavicle, to the left and right of the sternum. The teacher places the other hand on the student's navel. Optional: At the same time, an assistant slowly moves an object such as a pen, held 12 to 18 inches from the student's nose, from the student's left visual field to the right, and back again.*

The Brain Buttons activate the brain for:

- sending messages from the right brain hemisphere to the left side of the body, and vice versa
- receiving increased oxygen
- stimulation of the carotid artery for increased blood supply to the brain
- improved visual coordination
- increased grounding and centering

The Earth Buttons

The Earth Buttons help the learner to experience the connection between the body's upper and lower halves, thereby increasing coordination and stability. This activity brings the learner's attention to the lateral midline as a central point of reference, necessary for making decisions regarding the positions of objects in space. When the learner can organize her visual field in terms of her own body, her eyes, hands, and whole body become better coordinated. *The teacher rests both hands on the front lateral midline of the student's body. The fingertips of one hand rest under the lower lip; the fingertips of the other hand rest at any point between the navel and the upper edge of the pubic bone.*

The Earth Buttons activate the brain for:

- the ability to work in the visual, auditory, and kinesthetic midfield

- centering

- grounding, for such activities as walking down steps

- looking down to perform near-visual skills

The Balance Buttons

The Balance Buttons provide a quick balance for all three movement dimensions: left/right, top/bottom, and back/front. The restoring of balance that they provide to the occiput and the inner-ear area helps to normalize the whole body. *The teacher holds the student's Balance Buttons, located just above the indentation where the skull rests over the neck (about one and one-half to two inches to each side of the back midline, and just behind the mastoid area).*

177

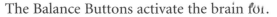

The Balance Buttons activate the brain for.

- increased proprioception for vestibular balance and equilibrium

- reestablishment of the body's gravitational center

- alertness and focus, by stimulating the semicircular canals and reticular formation

- improved head and neck alignment

- release of hyperactivity and hypervigilance

- changing visual focus from point to point

- relaxed jaw and cranial movement

- decision-making, concentration, and associative thinking

The Space Buttons

The Space Buttons help the learner to experience the connection between the body's upper and lower halves, thereby increasing coordination and stability. The grounding provided by this activity helps with spatial orientation. *The teacher rests both hands on the midline of the student's body—one above the upper lip on the front midline, the other on the back midline just above the tailbone. In some situations, the student may feel more comfortable if a higher point on the back midline is held.*

The Space Buttons activate the brain for:

- improved spatial orientation
- centering and grounding
- relaxation of the central nervous system
- ability to work in the visual, auditory, and kinesthetic midfield
- depth perception and visual contexts
- steadier eye contact
- near-to-far vision

The Energy Yawn

Yawning is a natural respiratory reflex that increases circulation to the brain and stimulates the whole body. Ideally, we should cover a yawn but avoid stifling it, which can create jaw tension. Yawning is good manners at the Brain Gym! *The teacher holds or gently massages any tense points on the student's jaw, especially over the rear upper and lower molars. This activity helps to balance the cranial bones and relaxes tension in the face and jaw. Together, the teacher and student make relaxed sighing sounds.*

The Energy Yawn activates the brain for:

- improved motor function for the muscles involved in mastication and vocalization
- increased respiration and oxidation of the blood for efficient, relaxed mental and physical functioning
- increased visual relaxation and centralization
- improved visual attention and perception
- more relaxed and coordinated movement of the facial muscles

179

- enhanced verbal and expressive communication
- increased discrimination of relevant from distracting information

The Thinking Cap

This activity helps the student focus attention on his hearing. It also relaxes tension in the cranial bones. *The teacher uses thumbs and index fingers to pull the student's ears gently back and then to unroll them. Begin at the top of the ear and gently massage down and around the curve, ending with the bottom lobe. Repeat three or more times.*

The Thinking Cap activates the brain for:

- crossing the auditory midline (including auditory attention, recognition, discrimination, perception, and memory)
- listening to one's own speaking voice
- short-term working memory
- silent speech and thinking skills
- increased mental and physical fitness
- hearing with both ears together
- switched-on reticular formation (screens out distracting sounds from relevant ones, releasing hyperactivity and hypervigilance)

Hook-ups

Hook-ups activate all of the balance-related muscles in the body, thus containing and stabilizing energy. The mind and body relax as attention returns to the core postural muscles and energy circulates through areas that were blocked by tension. The figure 8 pattern of the arms and legs (Part 1) follows the energy flow lines of the body. The touching of the fingertips (Part 2) balances and connects the two brain hemispheres. *The teacher helps the student to cross his arms over his chest (usually with the right arm on top), and to cross his ankles comfortably (usually with the left ankle on top). Hook-ups can be done sitting, standing, or lying down. The teacher holds the student's hands together, fingertips touching, for Part 2.*

Hook-ups activate the brain for:

- enhanced emotional centering

- grounding

- increased attention (stimulates reticular formation)

- release of hyperactivity and hypervigilance

- improved cranial movement

- increased respiration and oxidation of the blood

- improved balance and equilibrium

Part 2

Part 1

181

The Positive Points

The Positive Points bring blood flow from the hypothalamus to the frontal lobe, where rational thought originates. *The teacher lightly touches the student's forehead, resting fingertips on the points on the frontal eminences as illustrated, halfway between the hairline and the eyebrows and directly above each eye.*

The Positive Points activate the brain for:

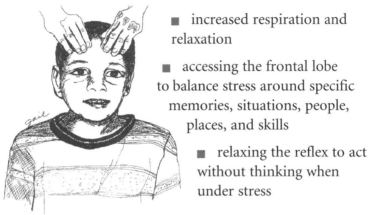

- increased respiration and relaxation

- accessing the frontal lobe to balance stress around specific memories, situations, people, places, and skills

- relaxing the reflex to act without thinking when under stress

The Midline Movements

The Midline Movements focus on the sensory skills necessary for each two-sided (left-right) movement that involves crossing the midline of the body. Thus, the Midline Movements help to integrate binocular vision, binaural hearing, and the left and right sides of the brain hemispheres as well as the musculature and symmetrical reflexes. The vertical midline of the body is the necessary reference for all such bilateral skills. The visual midfield (first defined by Dr. Dennison in *Edu-K for Kids*) is the area where the left and right visual fields overlap, requiring the paired eyes and all of their reciprocating muscles to work so well as a team that the two eyes function as one. Development of bilateral movement skills for crawling, walking, or seeing depth is also a prerequisite for whole-body coordination and ease of learning in the near-visual area. Bilateral coordination also impacts the child's growing sense of stability and autonomy.

Use of the movements helps to integrate neurodevelopmental reflexes related to laterality, including homolateral movements (those initiated and completed on one side of the body only); contralateral movements (independent cross-pattern movements of the arms and legs); and the ability to cross the midline for visual, auditory, or manual skills (for reading, for thinking and listening, or for writing).

The Cross Crawl

Because the Cross Crawl accesses both brain hemispheres simultaneously, this is the ideal warm-up for all skills that require crossing the body's lateral midline. In this contralateral exercise, similar to walking in place, the student alternately moves one arm and its opposite leg, then the other arm and

its opposite leg. *The Cross Crawl can be done lying down; the teacher motors the students through the movements. In a further adaptation, the student relaxes while the teacher alternately presses opposite hip and shoulder on the front or back of the body. These adaptations can also be done while the student sits, to relax the seated posture.*

This movement activates the brain for:

- coordination of core postural muscles
- ease of one-sided (homolateral) movements
- coordination of two-sided (contralateral) movements
- improved lymphatic stimulation, especially during times of excessive sitting
- crossing the visual/auditory/ kinesthetic/tactile midline

183

- left-to-right eye movements
- improved binocular (both eyes together) vision
- relaxed use of the diaphragm

Think of an X

The X symbolizes and evokes the brain-organization pattern for crossing the lateral midline. Ideally, through completion in infancy of a series of one-sided and cross-lateral developmental steps, the left hemisphere activates the right side of the body and the right hemisphere activates the left. Movement prepares the left and right hemispheres to work cooperatively, making both sides available for both receptive and expressive processes. The X is also a reminder of the Lazy 8, activating left and right brain hemispheres for both body movement and relaxation, and activating both eyes for binocular vision. *The X can be traced on the student's back, connecting opposite shoulder and hip.*

This movement activates the brain for:

- enhanced binocular vision
- centralized vision
- enhanced binaural hearing
- improved whole-body coordination
- relaxed use of the diaphragm and improved respiration
- enhanced postural awareness

Lazy 8s

The Lazy 8 (an infinity symbol lying on its side) includes a definite midpoint and separate left and right areas, joined by a continuous line. Drawing the 8 enables the reader to cross the visual/kinesthetic midline without interruption, thus activating both right and left eyes, integrating the right and left visual fields, and improving eye-hand coordination. *The teacher motors the student through the motion, always moving up the midline, then around and down. The Lazy 8 is drawn large, at eye level, with crayons or markers; or can be drawn in dry rice or sand, with finger paints, or with other visual/tactile mediums. Lazy 8s can also be drawn on the student's back to stimulate proprioceptive awareness.*

Lazy 8s activate the brain for:

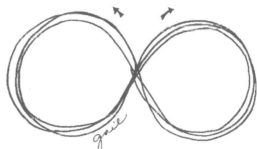

- crossing the visual midline for increased hemispheric integration

- enhanced binocular vision

- increased saccadic eye movements

- improved eye-muscle coordination (especially for tracking)

- improved eye-hand coordination

The Double Doodle

The Double Doodle is a bilateral drawing activity that is done in the visual-kinesthetic midfield to establish direction and orientation in space, relative to the body. The Double Doodle is best experienced with the large muscles of the arms and shoulders. *The teacher stands behind the student and motors her arms and hands through a few simple movements. The teacher says "Up, out, in, and down" while guiding the student to draw squares, circles, or other figures with both hands simultaneously. This teaches the student to refer to her visual/kinesthetic midline for directional reference. The teacher may stop motoring the student when both of her hands are able to move together, mirroring each other easily. Double Doodles can be drawn with such media as markers, crayons, fingerpaints, or shaving cream, or in sand or dry rice. Double Doodles can also be drawn on the student's back to simultaneously activate both brain hemisphere and stimulate proprioceptive awareness.*

This movement activates the brain for:

- enhanced binocular vision
- improved peripheral vision
- hand-eye coordination in different visual fields
- crossing the kinesthetic midline
- spatial awareness and visual discrimination

Alphabet 8s

Alphabet 8s adapt the Lazy 8 form to the printing of lower-case letters. This activity integrates the movements involved in the formation of these letters, enabling the writer to cross the visual midline without confusion. Each letter is clearly super-imposed on either one side or the other of the Lazy 8. A downstroke either ends the letter (for letters in the left visual field) or begins another letter (for those in the right visual field). For most students, when the printing of the lowercase letters improves, handwriting also becomes easier. *The teacher motors the student through the Lazy 8, then superimposes a lower case "a" in the left visual field. The Lazy 8 is repeated, then a "b" is superimposed in the right visual field. Clear distinctions are made between the letters in the left field, which begin with a curve, and those in the right field, which begin with a downstroke on the midline, then curve to the right.*

Alphabet 8s activate the brain for:

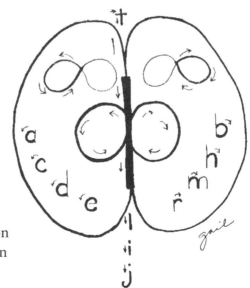

- crossing the kinesthetic/tactile midline for bihemispheric writing on the midfield

- increased peripheral awareness

- eye-hand coordination

- symbol recognition and discrimination

The Rocker

The Rocker releases the low back and sacrum by massaging the hamstring and gluteus muscle groups, stimulating nerves in the hips dulled by excessive studying, wheelchair sitting, etc., and freeing the sacrum. *The student sits on a padded surface. The teacher places one arm under the student's bent knees and the other around the student's shoulders. The student leans against the teacher; the teacher cradles the student and rocks him on one of his hips at a time, emphasizing small, circular movements to release the gluteal muscles.*

This movement activates the brain for:

- centering and the ability to work in the midfield
- grounding and stability
- left-to-right visual skills
- skills of attention and comprehension
- release of hypo- or hyperactivity and hypervigilance

The Energizer

The Energizer strengthens the forearms, neck, and chest muscles and encourages the student to use both eyes together in the visual midfield—all elements that prepare the learner for skills requiring fine-motor coordination. *The student rests on her belly, supporting her head and chest by placing her weight on her forearms. A rolled towel under the triceps gives necessary support.*

This movement activates the brain for:

- strengthened neck, chest, and forearms
- the ability to cross the midline
- a relaxed central nervous system
- binocular vision in the midfield

Additional Edu-K Processes Referred to in This Book

PACE: PACE is an acronym for Positive, Active, Clear, and Energetic — four qualities that we demonstrate when we are moving and learning at our own best rhythm and timing. In Edu-K, the four PACE activities help the individual to prepare for new activities by settling in to a comfortable learning pace. The PACE process consists of four simple Brain Gym activities: Water, the Brain Buttons, the Cross Crawl, and Hook-ups (referenced on page 78).

THE BRAIN GYM (EDU-K) BALANCE: A balance is a five-step educational process used in Educational Kinesiology (Edu-K) as part of a comprehensive personal development program. It brings movement and learning together in a profound system simply by following these steps: (1) get into PACE; (2) identify the action that represents the learning goal, the next incremental step in the learning process; (3) do a pre-activity; (4) do a learning menu from Brain Gym or other movement activities to activate the brain; and (5) repeat the pre-activity now as a post-activity, then celebrate and anchor the improvements (referenced on page 82).

189

THE GOAL WHEEL: The Goal Wheel, unique to Edu-K, is an empirical tool that assists the teacher in identifying and establishing an appropriate goal for the student. In Edu-K, the intention behind the goal is to integrate physical, mental, and emotional elements. In Cece's classroom, as is described in this book, the Goal Wheel is used with students who are unable to verbally express their wishes or goals (referenced on page 155.)

EDU-K IN DEPTH — SEVEN DIMENSIONS OF INTELLI-GENCE: This process addresses seven dimensions of intelligence as each relates to the whole mind-body system. Physical posture and body language are seen as correlates for brain organization, and each of the seven dimensions is an inter-relating system of structure and function in the brain-postural complex.

In Cece's classroom, the Seven Dimensions Balance is sometimes used for a child who appears to be seeking deeper or further integration, or when the Brain Gym movements alone seem to be insufficient.

VISION TRAINING: Vision training as used in Cece's classroom follows the model of the Creative Vision Balance, taken from the Edu-K In-Depth: Seven Dimensions of Intelligence course. Emphasis is on the underlying structural, muscular and electromagnetic functions related to deeply ingrained habits of eye usage and body posture. Visual skills are addressed by improving whole-body balance and coordination, and by integrating sensory modalities. When the vision training is indicated, it can be an opportunity to teach the eyes to function with less stress or tension. It can also be a powerful way to integrate movement and emotion at a higher level of function. Dr. Dennison discovered that new or less stressful visual patterns could be learned, often in a matter of minutes, by having the students hold certain points while doing exercises to enhance their visual skills. (The students in

Cece's classroom have these points held for them.) This system is unique to Edu-K. (*Edu-K In-Depth: Seven Dimensions of Intelligence Course Manual*, by Dennison and Dennison, 1995.)

DENNISON LATERALITY REPATTERNING (DLR): DLR (referenced on pages 83–84) is a wonderfully simple series of activities that coordinates both sides of the body in order to teach about crossing the body's midline. This crossing of the visual-auditory-kinesthetic midline enhances brain activity and whole-body organization by simulating the natural development of the infant during the creeping and crawling stage. For more information about DLR, see *Edu-K for Kids,* by Dennison and Dennison, 1987.

Bibiliography

Ayers, Jean. *Sensory Integration and the Child.* Los Angeles, CA: Western Psychological Services, 1979.

Ballinger, Eric. *The Learning Gym: Fun-to-Do Activities for Success at School.* Ventura, CA: Edu-Kinesthetics, Inc., 1996.

Batmanghelidj, F. *Your Body's Many Cries for Water.* Falls Church, VA: Global Health Solutions, 1993.

Cherry, Clare, Douglas Godwin, and Jesse Staples. *Is the Left Brain Always Right?: A Guide to Whole-Brain Development.* Belmont, CA: Fearon Teacher Aids, 1989.

Clark, Barbara. *Optimizing Learning.* Columbus, OH: Merrill Publishing Co., 1986.

Chopra, Deepak. *Quantum Healing: Exploring the Frontiers of Mind/Body Medicine.* New York, NY: Bantam Books, 1989.

Christopher, William and Barbara Christopher. *Mixed Blessings.* Nashville, TN: Abingdon Press, 1989.

Delacato, Carl H. *The Diagnosis and Treatment of Speech and Reading Problems.* Garden City, NY: Doubleday, 1974.

Dennison, Paul E. *Switching On.* Ventura, CA: Edu-Kinesthetics, Inc.,1981.

Dennison, Paul E. and Gail E. Dennison. *Brain Gym.* Ventura, CA: Edu-Kinesthetics, Inc., 1986.

Dennison, Paul E. and Gail E. Dennison. *Brain Gym Teacher's Edition*. Ventura, CA: Edu-Kinesthetics, Inc., 1989.

Dennison, Paul E. and Gail E. Dennison. *Edu-K for Kids*. Ventura, CA: Edu-Kinesthetics, Inc., 1987.

Dennison, Paul E. and Gail E. Dennison. *Personalized Whole Brain Integration*. Ventura, CA: Edu-Kinesthetics, Inc., 1986.

Doman, Glen. *How to Multiply Your Baby's Intelligence*. Garden City, NY: Doubleday, 1984.

Doman, Glen. *What to Do About Your Brain-Injured Child*. Garden City, NY: Doubleday, 1974.

Erickson, Joan. *Wisdom and the Senses: The Way of Creativity*. New York, NY: W.W. Norton & Company, Inc., 1988.

Gardner, Howard. *Frames of Mind: The Theory of Multiple Intelligences*. New York, NY: Basic Books, Inc., 1985.

Grammer, Red. *Teaching Peace*. Brooklyn, NY: Children's Group, Inc., 1986 (an audio cassette).

Grandin, Temple and Margaret Scariano. *Emergence: Labeled Autistic*. Novato, CA: Arena Press, 1986.

Hannaford, Carla. *Smart Moves: Why Learning Is Not All in Your Head*. Arlington, VA: Great Ocean Publishers, 1995.

Hannaford, Carla. *The Dominance Factor: How Knowing Your Dominant Eye, Ear, Brain, Hand, and Foot Can Improve Your Learning*. Arlington, VA: Great Ocean Publishers, 1997.

Hartmann, Thom. *Attention Deficit Disorder: A Different Perception*. Novato, CA: Underwood-Miller, 1993.

Hinsley, Sandra "Sam." *Brain Gym Surfer*. Stuart, FL: Hinsley & Conley, 1989.

Holt, John. *How Children Learn*. New York, NY: Pitman Publishing Co., 1969.

Kavner, Richard S., O.D. *Your Child's Vision: A Parent's Guide to Seeing, Growing, and Developing.* New York, NY: Simon & Schuster, Inc., 1985.

McCrone, John. *The Ape That Spoke: Language and the Evolution of the Human Mind.* New York, NY: Avon Books, 1991.

Pearce, Joseph Chilton. *The Magical Child Matures.* New York, NY: Dutton, 1985.

Piaget, Jean. *The Grasp of Consciousness: Action and Concept in the Young Child.* Cambridge, MA: Harvard, 1976.

Tortora, Gerard J. and Nicholas P. Anagnosstakos. *Principles of Anatomy and Physiology.* Sixth Edition. New York, NY: Harper, 1990.

Watson, Linda R. *Teaching Spontaneous Communication to Autistic and Developmentally Handicapped Children.* New York, NY: Irvington Publishers, 1989.

Williams, Linda Verlee. *Teaching for the Two-sided Mind: A Guide to Right Brain/Left Brain Education.* New York, NY: Simon & Schuster, 1983.

The following manuals, and the Educational Kinesiology Foundation courses for which they were written, provided a goodly portion of the research material for this book. The manuals are available, however, only to participants in the courses.

Dennison, Paul E. and Gail E. Dennison. *Creative Vision Course Manual.* Ventura, CA: Edu-Kinesthetics, Inc., 1987.

Dennison, Paul E. and Gail E. Dennison. *Edu-K Movement Reeducation Course Manual.* Ventura, CA: Edu-Kinesthetics, Inc., 1988.

Dennison, Paul E. and Gail E. Dennison. *Edu-K In-Depth: The Seven Dimensions Course Manual.* Ventura, CA: Edu-Kinesthetics, Inc., 1986.

Dennison, Paul E. and Gail E. Dennison. *Visioncircles Teacher's Manual.* Ventura, CA: Edu-Kinesthetics, Inc., 1987.

Stiller, Angelika and Renate Wennekes. *Sensory Stimulation Important to Developmental Processes Course Manual.* Neuenkirchen, Germany: Astrup, 31, 2846. 1992.

Stiller, Angelika and Renate Wennekes. *Motor Development Across the Body Midline Course Manual.* Neuenkirchen, Germany: Astrup, 31: 49434. 1996.